# DR. ALAN B. BIXLER

# TO BE OR NOT TO BE...
# BLESSED

Discover Blessings from the Mountain Perspective

# CONTENTS

# DEDICATION

To "*My Beautiful*" (Hef) Heather

"When God made you, He looked at me, and He saw how it would come to be, forever, together, God made you for me." I am truly blessed!

Love – Me

# INTRODUCTION

There are many blessings for followers of God.

*Deuteronomy 28:2-8*
And all these blessings shall come upon you and overtake you, if you obey the voice of the Lord your God. Blessed shall you be in the city, and blessed shall you be in the field. Blessed shall be the fruit of your womb and the fruit of your ground and the fruit of your cattle, the increase of your herds and the young of your flock. Blessed shall be your basket and your kneading bowl. Blessed shall you be when you come in, and blessed shall you be when you go out. "The Lord will cause your enemies who rise against you to be defeated before you. They shall come out against you one way and flee before you seven ways. The Lord will command the blessing on you in your barns and in all that you undertake. And he will bless you in the land that the Lord your God is giving you."

However, what does it mean to be blessed? When you do not understand it, there is a danger of missing out on everything God offers.

In the Sermon on the Mount, Jesus declares specific truths about what it means to be blessed. His message was directed to His closest followers who followed Him up the mountain, away from the crowds, to a higher, quieter place where they could hear His heart. What He revealed prepared them for what they would encounter as they moved the Gospel forward.

The sermon Jesus shared was challenging yet needed. The message on that mountain is as critical for Christians today as it was for His followers then. Like them, you must get away from the thoughts, experiences, and frenzy that goes on in the crowds.

You must go to a higher place to learn what true blessing is.

The Beatitudes are not a list of attitudes found in the Sermon on the Mount. They are descriptions of what it means to be blessed.

**Everything you need for your Christian walk is found in the Sermon on the Mount.**

*Matthew 5:1-12*
Seeing the crowds, he went up on the mountain, and when he sat down, his disciples came to him. And he opened his mouth and taught them, saying:

"Blessed are the poor in spirit, for theirs is the kingdom of heaven.
Blessed are those who mourn, for they shall be comforted.
Blessed are the meek, for they shall inherit the earth.
Blessed are those who hunger and thirst for righteousness, for they shall be satisfied.
Blessed are the merciful, for they shall receive mercy.
Blessed are the pure in heart, for they shall see God.

Blessed are the peacemakers, for they shall be called sons of God.
Blessed are those who are persecuted for righteousness' sake, for theirs is the kingdom of heaven.
Blessed are you when others revile you and persecute you and utter all kinds of evil against you falsely on my account. Rejoice and be glad, for your reward is great in heaven, for so they persecuted the prophets who were before you."

The message Jesus spoke was meant to empower, enlighten, and equip those closest to Him in advancing the Gospel forward. The message to Jesus' followers then and today is clear. No matter *what* you experience, you are blessed.

I hope you use this book as a measure and means for your Christian journey. The questions at the end of each chapter are meant to help you sift through self-reflection and life application challenges.

Just as Jesus' closest followers did on that mountain, I encourage you to dig deep, and in doing so, my prayer is that you know the full extent of His love for you and His blessings that are available to you.

*Ephesians 3:14-19*
For this reason I bow my knees before the Father, from whom every family in heaven and on earth is named, that according to the riches of his glory he may grant you to be strengthened with power through his Spirit in your inner being, so that Christ may dwell in your hearts through faith—that you, being rooted and grounded in love, may

have strength to comprehend with all the saints what is the breadth and length and height and depth, and to know the love of Christ that surpasses knowledge, that you may be filled with all the fullness of God.

# CHAPTER ONE – THE JOURNEY UP

## Facing the Mountain

*To be, or not to be that is the question.*
*Hamlet*

William Shakespeare wrote these famous words in *The Tragedy of Hamlet* sometime between 1599 and1602. That quote has become one of the most widely known and used in modern English history. [1] Far from being inspirational, they are the words of a troubled man reflecting on whether the right course was to escape his troubles through suicide or press on, living in his circumstance.

Although Hamlet is a fictional character, his moment of reckoning is commonly faced by Christians to some degree at some point in their life journey. Life today often brings difficulty, hardship, complexity, and distress. Many who find themselves navigating difficult life-storms, contemplate the same decision in varying contexts.

Even those whose lives have not brought life and death choices often experience moments where life seems to bring more trouble than good.

No one is immune to struggle, and most of us come to a place at least once in our lives when we choose to give up or continue believing by faith.

Christian or not, difficult times cause us to reexamine what we believe. It is at those times we ask ourselves, just as Hamlet did, whether or not our beliefs are enough to preserve us.

**The Simple Gospel**

In times of struggle, many Christians find themselves sorting through the depth of their belief. It is in those moments they question whether to be or not to be with Jesus. Problems cause even the faithful-strong to ponder whether it is better to live life through Jesus, or to take life into their own hands.

Ultimately, the question at the core of our Christian walk is whether or not to be in His presence.

Despite the depth of our questioning, the Gospel is really simple. The word itself means *good news*. It is a message of hope and redemption offered to all and unites a broken world to the God who created it. The opportunity we have with Jesus Christ is at the root of the question to follow or not. We miss the simplicity of the gospel when we choose our own path over His.

I join every other Christian who considers this question daily. We choose to be in God's presence and invite Him into what is going on in our lives or to live life relying on our own strength.

Bible scholars everywhere have spent lifetimes studying

the deep revelations of scripture. Still, there is value in studying the teachings of Jesus in their simplicity, so *we* better understand the perspective that there are things only God can do in our lives.

## A Growing Ministry

In Matthew chapter four, Jesus' influence was beginning to grow as He began transitioning into public ministry. As the story unfolds, it becomes evident that significant things were occurring.

*Matthew 4: 23-25*
And he went throughout all Galilee, teaching in their synagogues and proclaiming the gospel of the kingdom and healing every disease and every affliction among the people. So, his fame spread throughout all Syria, and they brought him all the sick, those afflicted with various diseases and pains, those oppressed by demons, those having seizures, and paralytics, and he healed them. And great crowds followed him from Galilee and the Decapolis, and from Jerusalem and Judea, and from beyond the Jordan.

Matthew's telling of the story shows us that Jesus had become quite famous, not only for His words, but for His actions as well. Everywhere He went, He spoke and lived in such a way that it astonished those who came in contact with Him. Commoners and wealthy alike heard and saw it.

Those closest to Him experienced it in deep personal ways. Even the religious leaders at the time began to recognize Jesus' ministry.

Wherever He went, a buzz sizzled through the crowd. People heard about Jesus and sought Him out. Many brought others to hear Him in hopes that He would heal the afflicted or sick. Some followed just to hear what He taught. As He walked through the crowds, excitement grew.

Most of the time, large crowds have a flow about them – it is often intense, and our senses are usually on overload. Try to imagine yourself as one of the people gathering around Jesus. Can you visualize how easy it would be to become overwhelmed by the frenzy of it all?

I believe most of us would easily be swept into the emotion of the masses. Yet even with the commotion of the people around Him, Jesus managed to remain focused as He saw to the needs of the people seeking healing.

There were some good things happening in the crowd. Healings and deliverance had caused Jesus' fame to spread all across the region. His ministry revealed a physical manifestation of what He offered spiritually. People who sought after the healing He offered were greatly impressed by His influence. It was powerful to be in His presence, and as He traveled the area, His following lingered near that power.

Eventually though, He moved on to the mountain.

Notice that the place Jesus went was not necessarily the easiest place to reach. The mountain was a place He went to separate from the masses and to get away from all the activity. The mountain was a place Jesus went for solace and focus, but in this case, a specific crowd followed. *That is significant.*

On the mountain, away from the everyday, they heard a deeper message about what it meant to be a follower of Jesus Christ. On the mountain, the message was deeper than what they experienced down below in the masses.

There is a lot going on in this story, and it is easy to get lost in the experience of the moment. But, if we take the time to dig in, what unfolds brings a revelation about what it really means to be close to Jesus and blessed.

**To be blessed with Jesus may cause you to make a choice between the masses or the mountain. It reveals the question of how close we want to be to Jesus.**

When presented with the question, most Christians would probably answer very quickly. Many would respond without giving it much thought. Some would even declare their desire to be closer to Him in a significant way. It is easy to answer without thought to the cost, but we should consider our answer carefully because many things occur when we get near to Jesus.

So, let's get close to Him and begin the climb.

**Climbing the Mountain**

The next chapter of Matthew's Gospel leads us into what is often referred to as "The Sermon on the Mount." We are introduced to the teachings Jesus shared from the mountain in the first verses of chapter five.

*Matthew 5:1*
Seeing the crowds, he went up on the mountain, and when he sat down, his disciples came to him.

In verse one we see that a specific group broke from the crowd and followed Jesus up the mountain.

It was likely a journey with some difficulty, but once there, His disciples came to Him. He sat down and began to open up a new perspective to them.

**To be blessed with Jesus may create questions about leaving the crowd to climb the mountain, and what it takes to endure an encounter with Him. Ultimately, how far are we willing to go with Jesus?**

Sometimes it is easier to follow Jesus with the masses than to follow Him up the mountain. In the crowd, we see up close and personal what He is doing in the lives of others. In the safety of the masses, there may be spiritual renewal and revival as we experience the miracles He does; however, it is outside the crowd that we often find Jesus uncovering deep layers of the realities of the Kingdom of Heaven for our personal lives.

Jesus saw the crowd and went to the mountain, and it was in *this* experience His disciples were positioned to encounter not only His message, but His presence and direction for their lives.

Matthew's account gives us insight into what many of us experience in our own lives. Perhaps it has been a little dry between you and Jesus.

Maybe there is a feeling of separation, and there seems to be distance in your relationship with Him.
It could be that you are struggling or find yourself wishing things were the way they used to be.

Sometimes our relationship with the Lord is like a seasoned married couple wishing they could go back to the way things were when they first fell in love.

We may have memories of great experiences with the Lord, but our Christian journey cannot be maintained on memories alone. In the end, the key to relational growth and change is what we choose to do with the opportunity to climb for higher ground or stay in the crowd.

In the book of Matthew, those who followed Jesus up the mountain were the ones who wanted to be close to Him. The gathering on the mountain had a very different experience than the crowd in the valley. The climbers took the more difficult path and were rewarded with a more profound understanding.

The crowd in the valley saw the miracles, but the people who climbed the mountain experienced the one who performed the miracles in a deeper way.

**To be blessed with Jesus may compel you to let go of the past in order to experience His presence. It reveals the need for a fresh perspective with Jesus.**

All Jesus did in the past was complete, and He was moving on. Only after a climb and beyond their past experiences would a mountain-moment with Jesus provide a higher level of understanding to His disciples.

What the masses had experienced by way of Jesus' miracles and ministry was tremendous. Amid all the great things He had done and the excitement of the crowd, Jesus went to the mountain. His reasoning reveals itself there, because He sat down to teach those who followed. After the climb, the ones who followed Him heard a message that would set the stage for their lives as they understood what it meant to be blessed.

**Often, we are called to make a choice between the masses or the mountain.**

Has Jesus ever done something in your life that caused you to question Him? Maybe you have experienced great victories, but now it seems like things are falling apart.

Perhaps you have found yourself asking where the Lord has gone. I think many of us have felt that way at some time or another.

Maybe some of those who followed Him up the mountain found the climb challenging and difficult. I am sure several wondered why they had to climb at all. It probably caused many of them to question Jesus' actions and motives.

They did not know that the lessons Jesus would teach them had to be experienced from another perspective and vantage point. It was going to require them to climb beyond the common ground. In order to appreciate what Jesus offered, they had to make a difficult choice. This new level of understanding meant they would need to remain in close proximity to Him. That meant *climbing*.

**Many times, it is easier to remain in the presence of the crowd than to climb toward the presence of Christ.**

Maybe the elevation is out of our comfort zone, or the way up is a bit too scary. Regardless, the mountain experience is the only way to get a completely different viewpoint of everything. It usually gives us greater perspective of what we are going to encounter, and it is on the mountain that we realize our complete need for Jesus.

**To fully experience what the Lord offers we MUST go to the mountain with Him.**

The crowds that followed Jesus then, are no different than the crowds that follow Him today. Some accepted what Jesus had to say, and some rejected what He had to say. Some received His offer for new life, and some, faced with difficult choices, turned away from His offer for new life.

Just like the people in Jesus' day, we come to Him for revival. That is certainly part of our Christian experience, but He has more to offer.

*He wants us to have mountain experiences, because it is there that He reveals things we cannot learn down in the valley.*

The mountain is where He shows us what is only available when we are closely connected to Him. Our eyes open in this connection, and our hearts are receptive to things we can never receive in the complications and craziness of the crowd. On the mountain, away from the masses, our motives and perspectives change.

The climb up is our choice alone. No Pastor can do it for us. No church can do it for us. It requires us to go on a journey that demands discipline and trust. We decide to either stay where we are, or put on our hiking shoes, go to the mountain, and experience what Jesus has for our lives.

## Questions

1. When you consider your relationship with Jesus, where have you chosen the masses over the mountain?

2. Where have you chosen the mountain over the masses?

3. When you consider your journey as a Christian, what things are barriers to a closer relationship with Jesus?

4. How do past experiences cause you to miss a fresh perspective of Jesus?

# CHAPTER TWO – BLESSING IN POSITION

## Blessings

If we were to take a survey, just about everyone – Christian or not – would likely say they want to be blessed. It does not matter how much we actually have, how comfortable our lives are, or how abundantly we have received, we seem to consistently desire more.

**The truth is, we often want more when we are actually already blessed more than we realize.**

*Blessing* is defined as God's favor, approval, or provision. In a Biblical sense, the word blessing invokes an understanding that with it, we receive much more than we could ever obtain for ourselves.

Many times, we equate blessing with things that are external. For some, it comes in the form of a job they love. For others it comes in the form of money, and the security of knowing they have a nest egg.

Countless people believe blessing is found in adventures, relationships, or possessions. In His mountaintop sermon, Jesus challenges those basic beliefs.
When Jesus began His public ministry, He taught and challenged people's understanding in many areas.

Through His public speaking and teaching, He set up expectations and built foundational understanding of belief in Him and His Kingdom. As He preached, miracles happened! People were healed, demons were cast out, and the individuals who followed Him received hope. It was an experience like never before. Jesus spoke to the heart of every issue, belief, and behavior – and His message was for every person.

**Jesus' ministry was exploding, and in the middle of the excitement, He saw the need for a mountain experience.**

*Matthew 5: 1-2*
Seeing the crowds, he went up on the mountain, and when he sat down, his disciples came to him. And he opened his mouth and taught them.

It is there on the mountain that Jesus begins to reveal the message that today is called the Beatitudes. The name of this sermon comes from the Latin word "beatus," which[2] means happy and blessed. Through that message Jesus reveals what it *really* means for His disciples then and now.

By the time we get to Matthew chapter five, those closest to Jesus have only known Him for a short time.

Try to imagine what it was like to be one of the disciples. Imagine the excitement of the face-to-face moments, seeing miracles, and watching Him bring life into circumstances where only death existed.

He brought healing where there was disease, deliverance

where the enemy was in control, and freedom from spiritual bondage for those held captive. So, the disciples probably came with expectations of a powerful revelation as they were astounded by His authority.

**When Jesus takes you up the mountain, be ready for something magnificent.**

Once up the mountain, Jesus sits down to teach. He intentionally begins His first sermon.

The words He speaks are foundational to everything else He teaches on and beyond the mountain. As His followers listen intently, He begins with these words:

*Matthew 5:3*
Blessed are the poor in spirit, for theirs is the kingdom of heaven.

Notice He does not say, "Blessed are the *poor*, for theirs is the Kingdom of heaven." It is easy to miss, but it is an important distinction. If He had said blessed are the poor, it would imply Jesus was speaking of something outwardly depressed.

On the contrary, someone who is poor in *spirit*, has an ongoing dependency that requires them to find strength through an inward knowledge of His Spirit beyond themselves or anyone else.

**To be blessed realizes possessions mean nothing, and Jesus means everything. It speaks to the spiritual *(inward)* rather than the physical *(outward)*.**

17

When Jesus says, "blessed are the poor in *spirit,"* He is talking about a disposition of character, and a revealing need for dependency on His spirit inside us.

In this statement though, Jesus clarifies blessedness in a way that is different and deeper. The difference is important to settle in our understanding or we may never truly experience what it means to be happy and blessed.

Jesus is not calling actual material poverty a blessed thing. It is about a call to live with a level of reliance on Jesus. We are instructed to live with an understanding that all help and strength comes through a relationship with Jesus Christ and His available Spirit.

Jesus was teaching that the one who recognizes the Lord as the *only* source of their strength, trust, and security is the one who is blessed. He was setting the groundwork for us to understand that blessing comes at an inward spiritual level and demands reliance on all things in God alone.

**Poor in Spirit**

When Jesus taught His message, the words He used were actually an exclamation which meant: "Oh how blessed are those who are poor in spirit" instead of being translated as blessed *are* the poor in spirit. [3] In other words, Jesus was declaring that we are blessed when we recognize our dependence on Him.

**To be blessed raises our dependence on the dependency of Jesus. It discloses how deeply we are willing to depend on Him.**

Dependence on God is not a new concept. There are many examples in the Old and New Testaments where reliance on God alone is declared. Jeremiah chapter seventeen speaks of the curse on someone who places their trust in a man or woman over trusting God. In Philippians chapter four, the Apostle Paul declares that God alone will supply all our needs through Jesus Christ.

Take the example of King David where there is a full account of his poor disposition and dependence on God.

*Psalm 62:5-12*
For God alone, O my soul, wait in silence,
 for my hope is from him.
He only is my rock and my salvation,
    my fortress; I shall not be shaken.
On God rests my salvation and my glory;
    my mighty rock, my refuge is God.
Trust in him at all times, O people;
    pour out your heart before him;
    God is a refuge for us. *Selah*
Those of low estate are but a breath;
    those of high estate are a delusion;
in the balances they go up;
    they are together lighter than a breath.

Again, the book of Psalms gives insight into understanding the kind of blessing that comes from complete reliance on God.

*Psalm 40:1-4*
I waited patiently for the Lord;
    he inclined to me and heard my cry.

He drew me up from the pit of destruction,
    out of the miry bog,
and set my feet upon a rock,
    making my steps secure.
He put a new song in my mouth,
    a song of praise to our God.
Many will see and fear,
    and put their trust in the Lord.
Blessed is the man who makes
    the Lord his trust,
who does not turn to the proud,
    to those who go astray after a lie!

Or here again where the Psalm describes a blessed person:

*Psalm 1:1*
Blessed is the man who walks not in the counsel of the wicked, nor stands in the way of sinners, nor sits in the seat of scoffers; but his delight is in the law of the Lord, and on his law he meditates day and night.

David understood the desperate need for dependence on God, in a deep, profound, and personal way. He was saying one is blessed when they recognize the Lord is the *only* source of strength, trust, and security.

**To be blessed is to recognize that obedience to Jesus proceeds possession of His Kingdom. It determines the requirements for experiencing blessing in God's Kingdom.**

When Jesus said, "*Blessed are the poor in spirit,*" He was

setting the foundational understanding that at the inward, spiritual level, reliance on God alone, in all things, is the only way one experiences blessedness.

The Kingdom of Heaven belongs to those who trust the Lord Jesus and are solely dependent on Him in their Spirit.

Blessed is the person who recognizes they do not have enough strength on their own. Blessed is the one who knows that hope is found *only* by trusting in God. Blessed is the one who recognizes that the Lord is the only source of power and security.

When Jesus said blessed are the poor in spirit, He was telling His disciples, and us, that reliance on God alone in all things is the only option for blessing. It is a critical concept because if we do not get that, nothing else will ever make sense, or ever make us happy and blessed.

What is profound about the exclaimed blessings of The Beatitudes is that they are not distant promises or future potentials. They are revelations of joy and happiness for today. The promise is for this time and this moment. It was for those who heard it then as much as it is for us now!

Still, we often equate poor with weak. In today's culture, our mindset is not to become weaker. Often our goal, and sometimes our prayer, is for God to make us stronger. On the surface that makes sense, but it is a double-edged sword, because it lessens our need for God. We think that if we are strong, we become capable. The truth is the exact opposite. If we are strong enough on our own, there is no need to go to God.

This is not a simple concept, but we also see it when Jesus teaches this same group of followers how to pray.

*Matthew 6:10*
Your kingdom come, your will be done, on earth as it is in heaven.

In the Lord's Prayer we ask for God's will to be done on Earth, just as in heaven. We are acknowledging that God is the pinnacle, above everything, and the King of all Kings. Still, sometimes we get that reversed and ask God to make *us* stronger. We tell ourselves that if God does this or that first, then we can bring glory to His name, but in the first statement Jesus made on the mountain, He says without Him you will never bring glory to God's name.

The message Jesus brings says that blessing is knowing that we are completely out of our league, that the fight is so much bigger than we can manage, and that we cannot possibly prevail on our own. When we put God in His rightful place, we are in agreement with the prayer, "As it is in heaven, so it is in Earth."

Jesus started His message by telling His disciples they had to be so poor in spirit, their only hope was in dependence on Him for it all. In doing so, that recognition would become the strength they needed to go forward.

## Rightful King Rightful Place

*Matthew 5:3*
Blessed are the poor in spirit, for theirs is the kingdom of heaven.

There is so much strength and power available when we recognize the true source of blessedness. However, if we want the power and access to the Kingdom, we must first submit to the King. If our desire is for true joy and happiness, we must first recognize our need for Jesus. If we want to be blessed, we must understand, Jesus is the source of such blessing.

The Apostle Paul explained what Jesus meant by being poor in spirit when He wrote to the Corinthian church. Paul was pleading with God because of his own weakness. He cried out to the Lord asking for the thorn in his flesh to be removed. But this reveals the unexpected way Jesus answers, and it is the key to blessedness.

*II Corinthians 12:9-10*
But he said to me, "My grace is sufficient for you, for my power is made perfect in weakness." Therefore I will boast all the more gladly of my weaknesses, so that the power of Christ may rest upon me. For the sake of Christ, then, I am content with weaknesses, insults, hardships, persecutions, and calamities. For when I am weak, then I am strong.

Jesus' first teaching statement to those closest to Him was the requirement to be poor in spirit. It is no different for us. If we want to experience blessing, then we too must position ourselves in such a way to gain all strength, direction, and hope through Him.

This is what it means to be strong, powerful, content, happy, and blessed!

## Questions

1. Where have you placed blessing contingent on outcomes or outward things?

2. Where have you trusted your inadequacies, shortcomings, or weaknesses to the strength and hope of Jesus?

3. What are the beliefs, misunderstandings, or fears that prohibit you from deep dependence on Jesus?

4. In what ways has reliance on your own strength kept you from possessing His Kingdom blessings in your life?

# CHAPTER THREE – BLESSING IN MOURNING

## Mourning Unfolded

The message Jesus spoke to His closest followers on the mountainside is as applicable today as it was then. What He revealed is life altering. It was powerful for the disciples, and if we are willing to go up the mountain, listen to His words, and apply them to our lives, we will be changed too.

*Matthew 5:1-3*
Seeing the crowds, he went up on the mountain, and when he sat down, his disciples came to him. And he opened his mouth and taught them, saying:
"Blessed are the poor in spirit, for theirs is the kingdom of heaven."

On the mountain Jesus taught that being poor in spirit is the realization that we are lowly and weak in our ability to alter our situation. When there is nothing in and of ourselves to give, we are poor in spirit. Jesus goes on to say that in recognition of our weak or poor state, we are blessed.

Therefore, we understand there is blessing when we

acknowledge our strength is not enough in any circumstance, or situation without Him.

The source of blessing is further unfolded as He reveals that it is attached to mourning as well.

*Matthew 5:4*
 Blessed are those who mourn, for they shall be comforted.

At first glance, that does not seem to make sense. Mourning is associated with hardship, hurt, or loss. Most people avoid things that are painful, and do whatever they can to resolve unpleasant things.

Still, despite how we feel about pain or discomfort, everyone experiences difficulties at some time in their lives. There is an array of things that get our attention.

Sometimes we are brought low by broken promises or relationships or because things have not turned out the way we expected. Other times we are faced with the loss of hope, direction, or purpose. Any of these experiences can trigger feelings of sorrow, regret, shame, or guilt.

Jesus teaches about something greater than sadness. He talks about sorrow at another level. Jesus describes a deeper experience within perceived loss. He speaks of something precious, and His words imply a personal connection that is available when there is loss of hope, direction, or purpose.

The word "mourning" has a deep spiritual significance in our lives. Mourning occurs at a deep level of our spirit. It is more profound than grief and can bring feelings of heaviness or darkness. It can cause us to feel physical pain, and often affects our emotions at a functional level. For some it brings complete and total depression.

## The Source of Comfort

As we reflect on the experience of deep loss, it is difficult from our own perspective to look at someone going through a season of mourning and come to the conclusion they are blessed. How is that possible? There on the mountain, Jesus is telling His closest followers that true spiritual comfort only comes through Him. To be encouraged when we are mournful requires the presence of Jesus.

**To be encouraged through difficulty emphasizes the presence of comfort in sorrow. It uncovers the need for intimacy with the source of His sufficiency in time of need.**

Remember, Jesus is speaking to His closest followers who have made the choice to follow Him up the mountain in order be near to Him. In this intimate setting, Jesus is giving them a deeper revelation of the blessing of His sufficiency, even in mourning.

He has explained there is blessing in being poor in spirit. And now He is telling them when they are mournful, comfort is available to them, and in that they are blessed.

Sometimes Christians struggle with the concept of trouble. People say things like, "I put my faith in Jesus, and now this horrible thing happened." Or they question God and wonder why they have to go through something difficult. But faith in Jesus is not about having an absence of sorrow.

**It is the understanding that regardless of what we go through, there is potential to find comfort in and through Jesus Christ.**

What Jesus offers to His disciples is an understanding of action. When they go through something so mournful, dark, and depressed that it may feel just a notch above death, they are blessed.

They had to take hold of the concept in order to be prepared for where they were going. It is a message we all need; however, not everyone wants or is ready to be comforted!

**To be empowered with comfort in weakness, we must express our weakness and embrace His strength.**

Just like a child in the middle of a tantrum, sometimes we are so angry, we refuse to be comforted. As a pastor, I have had a front-row seat at funerals where the loss of a precious loved one and the thought that things will never be the same causes people to become angry, even enraged. When that happens, the individual may push away from God's comfort as well. The problem with pushing it away, is that the possibility of blessing in mourning is also pushed away.

In reality, it is overwhelming to realize we are powerless to do anything about a situation. If you have ever stood at the casket of a loved one knowing you can do nothing to change the situation, you understand what it is to feel helpless. If you have ever watched someone make choices that result in unchangeable consequences, you know how impossible it can seem.

This was important enough that Jesus wanted His closest followers to understand it. And, He wants us to get it too. He wants us to recognize that even when we mourn, we are blessed, because we *will* be comforted.

Jesus' disciples were the ones who would carry the message of salvation to the world. Many were going to give their lives for the sake of the Gospel. All would find themselves in situations where they would be powerless to change the outcome. They needed to understand this, and so do we.

Jesus tells His disciples they are blessed and will be comforted when they are powerless, helpless, and poor in spirit. He reveals that when it is dark and depressing and the situation is overwhelming, they will be consoled. The message is that when we mourn, we are blessed, because powerful comfort and consolation is available.

Difficult and dark times are going to come for everyone. Even in those times we are blessed, because we have access to a comfort the world does not have. It can be a challenging concept to take in. But if this message was important enough to be part of Jesus inaugural sermon to His closest followers, then we should probably lean in too!

**We are not blessed because of the situation we are in. We are blessed because of the *one* who is in the situation with us!**

There is blessing when we realize we are powerless, helpless, and poor in spirit. When we have hit the deepest levels of mourning, we are also blessed because of the power and comfort that is available to us in Jesus. The Psalmist understood this aspect of blessing too.

*Psalm 121:1-2*
I lift up my eyes to the hills.
　From where does my help come?
My help comes from the Lord,
　who made heaven and earth.

Those closest to Jesus followed Him up the mountain to hear what He had to say. They came with expectation. And in that intimate experience, He teaches them about mourning, because He knows that if they do not understand this level of control, nothing else is ever going to make sense. It is something we also have to understand.

To receive the comfort Jesus offers, we have to have our own mountain time with Him. We can only understand the blessing of comfort and can only receive the power of control in our lives if we go up the mountain.

Maybe you are saying, "Lord I don't want to climb this mountain – I don't want to go there." You may think you do not have time to spend with Him or do not know if seeking mountain time is worth the effort.

Just like the Psalmist, we must look to the mountain.
We have to make the time to go up.

There may be many good things going on with the masses
down below. In the crowd you may see miracles and
deliverance. But on the mountain, Jesus is going to speak
some things into your life that you will not get without
climbing up.

What Jesus offers on the mountain is life altering. Even if
your life is overwhelming and you are poor in spirit, yours
is the kingdom of heaven.

Even in moments you feel a mournful and dark cloud, there
is comfort available to you. He is with you. He has not left
you, and He certainly has not forsaken you.

## Comfort Changes Us

**Comfort is not provided to change the *situation*; it is
there to change the person *in* the situation.**

This is important! What Jesus offers changes the person in
the midst of the circumstances. His ability to comfort is
described in a scripture many people are familiar with.

*Psalm 23:1-4*
The Lord is my shepherd; I shall not want.
He makes me lie down in green pastures.
He leads me beside still waters.
He restores my soul.
He leads me in paths of righteousness for his name's sake.

Even though I walk through the valley of the shadow of death,
I will fear no evil, for you are with me;
your rod and your staff, they comfort me.

This Psalm speaks about a reality that many of us will walk through at some time during our lives. The valley of the shadow of death in those verses seems pretty depressive and mournful. However, the Psalmist says we do not have to fear what is coming because the Shepard is with us, and His rod and staff *will* comfort us.

No matter what we go through, we can find comfort, because no situation is above God's ability to bring comfort to us.

**To embrace the purpose of comfort in loss confirms Jesus' intentions are to bless us beyond what we experience at the moment.**

One of the most familiar scriptures in all the Bible is:

*John 3:16*
For God so loved the world, that he gave his only Son, that whoever believes in him should not perish but have eternal life.

Mourning is the overwhelming realization that we have absolutely no control in and of ourselves. Repentance is a product of mourning which is a defining condition of salvation.

It is the absolute awareness and acceptance of our

depravity. In repentance, we acknowledge that without complete faith and reliance on Jesus, we are without the ability to escape the penalty for our sin.

**Jesus words of blessing correspond to the reality of mourning as it responds by faith in Him.**

When we profess Jesus as Lord of our lives, it means He is not just *over* everything, but that He *controls* everything. No one repents unless they are first mournful over their current state. It is more than being sorry; it is being sorrowful to the point that we are sickened at our disposition and character.

Jesus brought His closest followers up to the mountain to tell them, "You are not enough, but I am." He is offering them comfort that is only available through Him. And His comfort comes through repentance and acceptance. *This* is where blessing resides!

Our comfort is because of His power to control us. At a spiritual level, the comfort Jesus offers has the power to control our emotions, our responses, our reactions, our outlook, and our expectations. It keeps us in the right-mindedness of who is in power or control.

The Apostle Paul understood this control. He said:

*Philippians 4:13*
I can do all things through him who strengthens me.

**Comfort is not provided to change the situation; it provides His presence to the person *in* the situation.**

Jesus offers us the same thing He offered the disciples on that mountainside. He knew the situations they would face. He knew their circumstances would be overwhelming to them, and they would not have enough strength. And He knew we would *also* face those same moments.

Paul provides a description of Jesus' power in weakness.

*2 Corinthians 12:9*
But he said to me, "My grace is sufficient for you, for my power is made perfect in weakness."

When we lose all hope of our control over the desired outcome and cry out, "Lord your will be done," that is when we are blessed. However, we have that comfort *only* when we recognize the source is only through Jesus.

*Acts 17:28*
"'In him we live and move and have our being."

It does not matter what situation we are in, and it makes no difference who made the decisions that brought us there. We are blessed because we have a Savior who is for us – not against us. In Him, we find blessing beyond our situation.

Mourning brings with it, the need to be encouraged, empowered, and embraced.

Jesus provides His presence, power, and purpose into our experience of mourning.

In Matthew 5:4, Jesus is saying we are blessed because

we will be comforted. It is a powerful offer, but that comfort only comes through the recognition of His ultimate power and control.

## Questions

1.  When have you turned (or not turned) to Jesus as the source of comfort in a difficult time?



2.  How is recognition of your weakness crucial to receiving blessing?



3.  When has a difficult experience changed you? How?

# CHAPTER FOUR – BLESSING IN MEEKNESS

Up until they reached the mountain, Jesus had been ministering to the people who followed Him. It was a powerful and extraordinary time. His fame had spread, and people had come from all over the region to see and hear Him speak. To some, it might seem like His ministry was reaching its pinnacle, but He was only beginning.

First, Jesus tells His disciples that there is blessing when they are poor in spirit because in poverty of spirit, theirs is the Kingdom of Heaven. He then reveals that they are blessed when they mourn because they will be comforted. Now, He takes them even deeper.

On the mountain, they listen as He tells them that when they are meek, they are blessed.

*Matthew 5:5*
Blessed are the meek, for they shall inherit the earth.

**Power Under Control**

Meekness can be described as power under control. However, that definition can miss the deeper meaning.

37

In His message, Jesus points out the meek are blessed, not just when they trust His control, but when they *do not* have power. This blessing requires that they also trust Him for things they *do* have power over.

**Meekness is trusting the outcome to God when it is within your power to influence or change the circumstances.**

Remember, right before this, Jesus told His disciples there is a blessing of comfort when they mourn. It is interesting that Jesus revealed that concept right before He began talking about meekness since mourning is usually related to the inability to control the outcome of a circumstance.

**Meekness is the willingness to let go of the outcome when we *can* control the circumstances.**

Our willingness to allow control is frequently based on our comfort with someone else's ability to influence the outcome of a situation. At a spiritual level, our biggest struggles are often with issues of control. Many times, our trust in God is directly related to the level of control we feel most comfortable allowing Him to have.

The difficulty in navigating struggles, often relates to the aspect of *who* has control in our lives. Many times, as Christians, we will say that Christ rules our lives, but frequently there is a battle for full control.

**To experience His blessed control is an issue of self-control versus God-control. It determines the level of trust we have in Him.**

To be or not to be meek is a question of *who* is taking control, grabbing hold of the steering wheel, or who will hold the course. Blessing is in the balance.

When we are a passenger in a car, someone else is driving. Most of us would say the person in the driver's seat has control of the car. However, the passenger does have the option to reach over, grab the wheel, and create... a moment.

That is often how our Christian journey goes too. Many times, we struggle because trust in God's ability to take us through difficult or challenging places is as much a matter of allowing Him to have control as it is giving up ours.

One illustration I have heard over the years to explain meekness is that of training a wild horse, or Mustang. When the horse is broken, you are able to harness, saddle, and ride it. But that animal still has all the power it ever had. It still has the potential to do what it did before it was broken. What is different is that now its power is harnessed and under control. That is a great example of meekness

When someone makes Jesus Lord of their life, they give Him complete control. Meekness is the ultimate humbling and submission of all controls.

That perspective can be difficult for us. In some ways it is just like being a passenger in someone's car. Even though we can grab that wheel, we consciously make the choice not to. We determine to put our trust in the one who is in the driver's seat.

Jesus told those who followed Him up the mountain that with meekness, there is a blessing of inheriting the earth. That is an enormous promise! Yet it is so much deeper than inheriting real estate, because meekness implies power. The question is, whose power?

At a deep level, meekness is an understanding that on our own, we lack the authority needed for any situation. It is about the state of our faith condition, and the power offered requires us to give God lordship over everything – the things we cannot control, *and* the things we can. When we understand and accept that, Jesus says we are blessed.

**Mountain Ways**

Many times, God's response to a situation is very different than ours – especially if in our minds, we have the power to influence the outcome. Meekness does not only encompass only the things I am powerless to change. Meekness comes into play when we are able to say, "Lord your way and your will be done, even in the things I can influence." That is what the meekness Jesus reveals to his followers looks like.

**To be contained in His blessing reveals the struggle between my ways versus mountain ways. It discloses the root of pride.**

Often the issue of control is connected to pride. Meekness means setting aside our own ability and looking to God's control in *all* things.

It is the perspective that regardless of our ability to affect the result of any situation, God ultimately controls the outcome.

It is a sobering thought to submit ourselves under complete control. As humans we often rebel against full submission to another. Pride does not consider God's authority, and prefers self-will to God's will. To be contained by meekness is to be aware of boundaries that may cause our way to oppose Jesus' mountain way.

Pride is a disposition to exalt self above God. Sometimes we excuse it as a matter of personality. We use words and concepts like "strong-willed," or say things like, "it's just who I am," and, "That is just how I have always done things." Other times we justify pride by concealing it as caring. Saying things like "I just want to make sure everything is fair and everybody is happy with the process, decision, or direction."

Then there are those whose pride is exposed through their behavior. They may falsely believe their survival must be protected by outbursts and reactions. Even when the reaction does not change the circumstance or the person is not right, the feeling is, "At least I have been heard." It is the opposite of trusting God.

*1 John 2:16*
For all that is in the world—the desires of the flesh and the desires of the eyes and pride of life—is not from the Father but is from the world.

Whatever the external behavior or excuse for not having meekness, pride is at the root of the problem. Pride opposes what Jesus taught about meekness. It results when we are defined by who we are, rather than *whose* we are.

Peter is the disciple who knows better than anyone what it is to put his foot in his mouth. We see throughout the Gospels where pride causes Him to fail many times, even though He was one of those closest to Jesus. Yet in His first letter, Peter speaks what he learned about letting the Lord control life.

*1 Peter 5:6-7*
Humble yourselves, therefore, under the mighty hand of God so that at the proper time he may exalt you, casting all your anxieties on him, because he cares for you.

Peter personally knew that God opposes the proud but gives grace to the humble. He was there when Jesus disclosed that message to those who followed Him up the mountain. When God is in control of our lives there cannot be any element of pride.

Pride and complete surrender cannot co-exist. We cannot say, "Lord Jesus, I make you Lord of my life," and then when a difficult situation arises take matters into our own hands. God's ways usually do not look like ours. Therefore, if we struggle with the way He does things, we are not fully under His control.

When we relinquish all control to Him, we make Him Lord of our lives.

To be meek is to set aside any reliance on self, and to submit to God's control over all things in our lives - not just in the small things, not just the big things, but in all things. It is a struggle between my ways and mountain ways.

*Romans 12:1-2*
I appeal to you therefore, brothers, by the mercies of God, to present your bodies as a living sacrifice, holy and acceptable to God, which is your spiritual worship. Do not be conformed to this world, but be transformed by the renewal of your mind, that by testing you may discern what is the will of God, what is good and acceptable and perfect.

My ways conform me to the world; but Jesus' ways transform me to *His* way. My ways lead to envy and strife, but Jesus' ways produce an everlasting inheritance for me as I wait for Him.

The meek let the Lord control and contain them through every trial, in every circumstance, and in every decision. They yield to His lead, because they know Him and trust Him at His Word.

Meekness allows God to set us apart from the world, and in so doing, we receive what only He can give.

Jesus went to the mountain, because what He had to teach His disciples was deeply important. It could not be understood in the frenzy of normal, everyday life. He knew what He was about to teach them was critical. They had to understand that blessing is beyond circumstance, beyond feelings, and beyond what they could see.

**To be consecrated before the Lord is a battle of self-righteousness versus God's righteousness. It determines blessing in the outcome.**

What Jesus shared on the mountain was preparing His disciples to be consecrated, set apart for His purpose, and positioned to demonstrate His power in their lives.

When we are meek, humble, and patient before the Lord, He causes things to move, change, conform, or be contained in and to His will.

When God uses us, we must remain humble. Remember, meekness is about power under control. It is allowing God to harness our power, while His power remains in its proper place.

It is easier, more natural, to operate more in our own power than His. We often want things to happen in our own time, and in our own way. But we learn how to be meek and patient when the Lord causes things to move at a different pace. It is then He changes us. It is in following His lead that we learn meekness.

There are so many times our prayers get ahead of the Lord. Perhaps we are in a difficult situation, so we cry out and ask Him to show up and do *something*. Usually the meaning behind that prayer is if God does not do something, we will. That is not meek, and can get us into trouble.

We can get ahead of God when we do not wait for Him, but when we trust, amazing things happen.

King David wrote about trusting God's timing. In fact, in this Psalm He reveals his understanding of meekness.

*Psalm 37:7-11*
Be still before the Lord and wait patiently for him; fret not yourself over the one who prospers in his way, over the man who carries out evil devices! Refrain from anger, and forsake wrath! Fret not yourself; it tends only to evil. For the evildoers shall be cut off, but those who wait for the Lord shall inherit the land. In just a little while, the wicked will be no more; though you look carefully at his place, he will not be there. But the meek shall inherit the land and delight themselves in abundant peace.

The meek will inherit the land because they let the Lord encompass them through every trial, and in every decision. They know and trust the Lord at His word. Meekness is the only thing that allows for God to set us apart from the world. And in setting us apart, we receive the blessing only *He* can give.

Meekness is realizing we will never be able to change any situation or circumstance on our own, but when we put Jesus at the helm of our lives, we are blessed.

**To experience contentment is an attitude of self-rightness versus Godly rightness. It discloses gratitude in the moment.**

When I was a kid, my grandpa would sometimes offer me what he called a "deal." He would call me over to him and tell me he had a deal, then he would hand me a twenty-dollar bill. When I was young, that was a lot of money.

However, when I got older, I started to think I needed more. Eventually, I got ahead of grandpa and told him I had a deal for *him*, and it involved him giving me another twenty dollars. Of course, he promptly turned me down. Ha!

It is funny now, but there is a lesson in that experience. Sometimes God gives us a deal and we are grateful. Other times we see it from the wrong perspective. We think we need more, and because of that, we miss the greatness of what God is truly offering to us.

*It works like this*: if God makes us strong, then in reality we do not need Him to make us stronger. If He makes us wise, we do not need Him to make us wiser. *In everything*, we just need to lean into what is available to us through Him and trust that it is enough.

Contentment through meekness involves power that allows control to the point that I do not question the Lord or His ways. It means I live in such a trusted place that whatever happens, I am blessed, because I am content. That is a powerful, and beautiful place to be!

So how is this accomplished in everyday life? Jesus gives us the answer a few chapters later in the book of Matthew.

*Matthew 11:29-30*
Take my yoke upon you, and learn from me, for I am gentle and lowly (meek) in heart, and you will find rest for your souls. For my yoke is easy, and my burden is light.

Yokes are placed on oxen, not to hurt them or add extra weight, but to control them. Yokes provide the assurance of guidance by the one who holds the reins and understands the bigger purpose.

When Jesus says take my yoke upon you, He is telling us not to be controlled by anything other than Him. The implication is not just of control. It implies we have a lighter burden as we rest in His ability to guide.

Jesus knew the distractions and temptations we would face. There are so many things that easily compete for control over us, and cause us to go off track, but if we are yoked with Him, He steers us to the right place at the right time.

I understand sometimes there is a power struggle. We may want to go left when Jesus is turning right. When we are meek in heart, we yield to His leading. Contentment is found when we take His yoke upon us.

The yoke is an example of power under control. The Lord knows the best way, and there is blessing in His direction. Under His yoke, we inherit the earth, find rest for our souls, and are blessed.

**The meek are blessed because they put everything at the feet of Jesus.**

In being meek before the Lord, we are blessed when we are controlled by God, contained in His ways, consecrated for works of righteousness, and content in our lives.

47

When we honor the Lord with the obedience of meekness, He will honor us with an everlasting inheritance! It means we are in such a trusted place that whatever happens we are blessed because we are content.

Those who follow Him up the mountain learned a deeper understanding of blessedness. And in the Beatitudes, Jesus says blessed are the pour in spirit, blessed are the mournful, and blessed are the meek.

All of these are bound together with an amazing result. We get an inheritance! Not because we *deserve* it, since that would be because of our own righteousness. It is because we are meek before the Lord and He makes Himself available, in that we are blessed.

## Questions

1. Where have you relied on "self" rather than trusting in God's control?

2. Where have you relied on God's control and saw His blessing?

3. In what ways has pride played a part in the struggle to lean into God's control?

4. When has self-righteousness caused you to take matters into your own hands?

5. How can meekness change your gratitude for the things God has done?

# CHAPTER FIVE – BLESSING IN RIGHTEOUS HUNGER AND THIRST

## Appetite or Craving

Cravings are a fascinating phenomenon.

During pregnancy, many women say they have experienced cravings, and there are some pretty peculiar examples out there. That was certainly the experience my wife Heather had when she was pregnant with our oldest.

One of the strangest cravings she had was for supreme deep-dish pizza. On its own, that is not such an unusual request. What made it so odd, was that she covered it in maple syrup and gobbled it up! I still remember the syrup dripping over the sides. She thought it was delicious. But I remember gagging at the thought of eating it, even though it was a craving for her.

Maybe like me, you would *never* consider eating something like that. However, if we were starving, and supreme deep-dish pizza with maple syrup was the only thing available, we would probably be quite happy to eat it. Our appetite changes when cravings are replaced with starvation. As humans, hunger *and* thirst are two of our greatest needs.

Long term survival depends on both. Without food we die of starvation. Without water, we die of dehydration. Unless *both* are satisfied, we are in a desperate condition.

These dependencies of hunger and thirst are not *just* related to food. There is a spiritual aspect, and spiritual hunger and thirst provide what we need for our life of faith.

## Spiritual Hunger and Thirst

Jesus is teaching His closest disciples what it is to be blessed. If the disciples do not understand what it is to be blessed at a deeper level, they will miss the big picture of what it is to truly be followers of Christ.

He taught them what it means to be blessed when they are poor in spirit, when they are mournful, and when they are meek. Now He reveals there is blessing in the area of their appetite.

*Matthew 5:6*
Blessed are those who hunger and thirst for righteousness, for they shall be satisfied.

Jesus addresses satisfaction from the standpoint of hunger and thirst to teach His followers that blessing is not determined by circumstances.

What He reveals was as applicable to His disciples then as it is to us now. This teaching could be interpreted as radical because starvation and blessing seem contrary to one another.

What He was saying was outside how we typically think. Even today, many have trouble with this concept.

**To be blessed and satisfied appeals to our appetite. It discloses the need for spiritual nourishment.**

Jesus says that those who hunger and thirst for righteousness will be satisfied. In order to understand the meaning behind what He is saying, it is important to look more deeply at the words He uses. The words for hunger and thirst used in verse six of Matthew chapter five, have a contextual implication that impacts the meaning.

The passage is referring to a need that cannot be satisfied with just a bite of bread, or a swallow of water. The kind of hunger Jesus describes is so big, the only way to satisfy it is with the whole loaf. And the level of thirst He defines requires the whole pitcher of water to satisfy.[4] The full translation would be, "Blessed are those who hunger and thirst for the whole, complete, and total righteousness of God. If there is anything less, you will not be satisfied!"

In our culture it can be difficult to wrap our minds around that logic, but Jesus is teaching His closest followers something that is so profound it has potential to carry them through life. We need to grasp the concept as well.

Jesus reveals that righteousness, completion, wholeness, virtue, and justice, in the area of both hunger and thirst are what bring full satisfaction. Righteousness in one area alone brings, at best, survival for the moment.

### Survival or Satisfaction

Survival and satisfaction are completely different things. Survival connotes a need that cultivates continued existence, while satisfaction is the fulfilling of a need, desire, or appetite.

Jesus' use of the word satisfaction implies the result is enough, or a complete filling.

If my hunger and thirst are not addressed, I am in a desperate situation. Jesus uses these primary needs to illustrate what it means to truly be satisfied in a spiritual framework. That satisfaction is in the context of *His* righteousness.

**To be blessed and satisfied appeals to our alternatives. It reveals the potential to settle for other options over the things of God.**

Everyone has both physical and spiritual appetites. Just as we all have different preferences when it comes to food, we sometimes look for alternatives and options when it comes to our spiritual life.

A lot of people have an appetite for the spiritual things; however, some only want certain parts of what God offers. Many crave the wrong things, or only want a little taste. The problem is, anything less than full satisfaction of what God offers spiritually will leave us lacking.

*There are ways to tell when we have settled for less than everything God offers.*

Perhaps you are going through something, and you wonder where God is in the situation. Maybe He seems a little distant. If you are feeling spiritually drier than you want to be or like something is alluding you, it could be that you are just tasting, just nibbling, just taking a sip of the things of God.

He is offering a full menu, but you may be settling for an

appetizer rather than the full buffet. If you feel like you are just surviving spiritually, it could be a matter of your appetite.

What Jesus offers is the opportunity to fill ourselves with the entire spiritual potential available to us. Therefore, when it comes to your appetite, this righteousness deals with fulfillment in both areas of hunger and thirst. Jesus is talking about righteousness attached to blessing, which ultimately satisfies your whole being.

This is important! When Jesus says we are blessed when we hunger and thirst for His righteousness, the requirement is to take all He offers, not just a taste.

When we hunger and thirst for all He has to offer, there is a blessing attached to it, because we are satisfied. When every other life alternative is set aside, and our complete expectation is placed in Him and His ways, that is righteousness.

**To be blessed and satisfied appeals to our absolutes. It divulges our true appetite for the things of God.**

Absolutes are statements that assume what is said is true one hundred percent of the time. For example, "If you jump off the roof of a two-story building, you will fall to the ground."

Sometimes people set up these kinds of absolutes in their spiritual lives.

They may say things like, "If God was in this, He wouldn't have allowed that," or "I will do such-and-such, if God does this for me," or "If the Lord is in this, it will feel comfortable."

We have to be careful, because blessing is not attached to the outcome of *any* situation. It is not attached to expectations, what God gives us, or what He does not. Blessing is only attached to a relationship with Him. And because of that relationship, no matter what happens to me or around me, I am blessed because of the *One* who is with me.

Up on the mountain Jesus wanted His disciples to know that He was going to be with them and would never leave or abandon them. He wanted them to understand this concept, because a lot of truly great things were going to happen to them. But a lot of hard things were going to happen, too. They needed to grasp this, and we do too.

What we want and how bad we want it are all tied to our absolute beliefs, and the only absolute we can have is this:

**Jesus is not *just* the best way; He is the *only way*.**

**To be blessed and satisfied appeals to craving versus starving for righteousness. It determines the level of hunger for the things of God.**

Jesus explained hunger and thirst to His disciples in relation to craving versus starving for righteousness.

Starving and craving are two very different concepts. If we are starving, our focus is on life and living. When we are truly starving, we do not care about anything but filling the need for whatever is necessary to sustain life.

> *Starving* focuses on life and living.
> *Craving* focuses on likes and luxury.
> *Starving* is about desperate dependence.

*Craving* is about distinguishing delicacies.
*Starving* is about choosing to live.
*Craving* is about living to choose.

## The Value of Desperation

Everyone needs to get to the point where they can say, *"God, I am desperately dependent on everything you have for me, however little or much. It doesn't matter Lord; I'll take whatever you have for me."*

When we are desperately hungry and thirsty for Jesus' righteousness, our focus is on the life *He* has for us, not the one we made for ourselves. Our entire future and life are blessed when we are at the point of spiritual starvation and are willing to abandon everything to Jesus as the only source of sustenance.

We are blessed when we make Him Lord of our lives, and do not need a say in the choices or outcome of any situation. Just like Paul in his letter to the Romans, we are blessed when we can say:

*Romans 8:31*
If God is for us, who can be against us?

If we look at Matthew 5:6 in the context of our cultural logic, it does not make sense. Jesus is saying it is not just where we find *sustenance*, it is where we find *satisfaction*. And if we find satisfaction in Him alone, that is when we are blessed.

That is powerful and incredible news, church!

Recently I came across an article[5] that illustrates what

Jesus was saying so well. It said that when people are dying, they typically lose their sense of hunger or thirst. That really struck a chord for me, because I learned a long time ago that many times there is a physical manifestation of what happens in the spiritual.

Over the years I have seen this played out. When someone's spiritual life dies, they often lose their appetite for the things of God. They may have no clue it is happening. They just know things are not the way they used to be. Just like someone in the process of dying, their appetite has changed, and their spiritual hunger and thirst are deadened.

Maybe the appetite you had early in your Christian journey has changed. All of a sudden you find yourself looking for alternatives to fill your desires. Perhaps you have started developing absolutes and dictating to God your prayers. All of this accumulates, and we wonder why our appetite for God's righteousness declines.

When we are sick, doctors often encourage us to continue trying to eat and drink in order to avoid further physical decline. We understand this in the physical, but somehow it escapes us in the spiritual.

When we do not hunger and thirst for the things of God, it is a symptom that our spiritual life is dying.

Sadly, I believe when people experience spiritual death, many are completely unaware that it is happening. The reality is Jesus knew those times would come for all of us. His lesson to the disciples on that mountain told them how to avoid spiritual death, and that message is for us too.

The truth is there are going to be difficulties in our lives. Struggle is beneficial, because it causes us to feel spiritually hungry and thirsty. We must recognize that His righteousness, and ways are higher than ours. When we understand that, regardless of what happens, we are blessed!

To access that blessing, we just have to respond to Him.

The Lord says He is at the door.

*Revelation 3:20*

Behold, I stand at the door and knock. If anyone hears my voice and opens the door, I will come in to him and eat with him, and he with me.

We have to take action. Open the door instead of leaving Him outside. Draw close, and take more than just a bite of the bread and a sip of the water Jesus has for us. When we take hold of the whole loaf, the whole pitcher, we are blessed – beyond feeling, beyond situation, and beyond what anyone else does or provides.

The Savior wants to come in and wants you to realize He's more than enough. What He has is more than enough for you, if you take it *all* in.

That is a blessing, church, and it is available to us!

Scripture gives us a picture of what it looks like to hunger and thirst for the Lord. Here, the psalmist writes:

*Psalm 421-2*
As a deer pants for flowing streams,

so pants my soul for you, O God.
My soul thirsts for God,
for the living God.
When shall I come and appear before God?

I cannot help but think we all need this reminder. If you are overwhelmed, exchange your cravings for the things of God. If there is something missing, and you do not feel fulfilled, be satisfied with everything God offers.

If we hunger and thirst for *His* ways and *His* righteousness, we will be fulfilled, sustained, and satisfied with our lives.

## Questions

1.  Where have you settled for less than the full spiritual blessings of the Lord?


2.  What spiritual alternatives have you settled for?


3.  Where have you allowed absolutes to slip into your spiritual life?


4.  Describe the difference between craving versus starving for righteousness,

# CHAPTER SIX – BLESSING IN MERCY

## The Game of Mercy

Perhaps some of you are familiar with the game of "mercy." If not, here is how it works.

In the game, two challengers face each other and join hands, with finger and thumbs interlocking. On the word *go*, each player attempts to bend back the opponent's hands and inflict pain by straining their wrists. When a player can no longer stand the pain, they declare defeat by shouting "Mercy!"

Mercy is a game of strength, skill, endurance, and pain tolerance. Some consider it a fun game… that is until faced with an opponent who is exceptionally stronger. Still, even when players are evenly matched, at some point someone eventually cries *mercy*.

In the spiritual realm, mercy often plays out the same way. In the game, the idea is to use all of one's power to overcome the other person. Spiritually, we interlock ourselves with God as well. The difference between playing with God or each other, is that in *every* match, His strength has the potential to destroy us.

Thank goodness we have a loving and merciful God.

*Lamentations 3:22-23*
The steadfast love of the Lord never ceases; His mercies never come to an end.

The good news for us is when we get down on our knees and cry mercy, He is compassionate – even when we actually do not deserve it because of sin.

## Mercy Defined

As Christians, we often talk about mercy's benefit to us. We say things like, "I just need God's mercy," or "I need Him to show some mercy in my life."

But what does it really mean when we ask for mercy?

In the game, the one who cries *mercy* has submitted to defeat. In effect, the person is tapping out, much like a fighter. In that context, mercy is the acknowledgment of weakness, but that viewpoint is flawed from a spiritual standpoint.

Mercy from God's perspective is not about our acknowledgement of weakness. In crying out for *God's* mercy, we are actually acknowledging His *power*.

Biblical mercy deals with the admission, or recognition, that the exercise of power in His capable strength will not be utilized.

That is mercy! *That* mercy is strength and power under control.

## Blessing in Mercy

The mountain message was foundational. Away from the crowds, with His closest disciples, Jesus explained what it means to be blessed.

The message was vital to them, because some would ultimately give their lives for the gospel. In order to face those experiences, they needed to understand a deeper revelation of God's blessing.

Jesus' sermon revealed that there is blessing when they are poor in spirit, when they mourn, when they are meek, and when they hunger and thirst for righteousness.

Now, He takes them further into the understanding of blessing.

*Matthew 5:7*
Blessed are the merciful, for they shall receive mercy.

Jesus tells the disciples that mercy has a blessing attached to it, but the deeper lesson was that in order to receive the blessing, they had to *be* merciful. If they were not, they would not *receive* mercy, and therefore would not be blessed.

## Mercy Over Judgment

The true meaning of mercy is not about giving and taking. It is about giving and receiving. There is a big difference. *The power* of mercy is in the blessing, and the *blessing* is in the acknowledgement of God's power.

Jesus' brother, James, writes about mercy.
*James 2:13*
For judgment is without mercy to one who has shown no mercy. Mercy triumphs over judgment.

Mercy triumphs over judgment! Judgment crushes and destroys, where mercy shows compassion and forgiveness.

Have you ever arm-wrestled a child? When our son Hunter was about six years old, he sometimes challenged me to arm-wrestle. Every time, he would use every ounce of His strength to try to pin my arm. I could have slammed His hand to the table. I had the option to use my power to either crush him or let him win.

At a spiritual level, that is what God does with us.

Occasionally Christians will state that the Bible says not to judge, but it does not say that! It actually says we will be judged using the same measure we use to judge others.

*Matthew 7:2*
For with the judgment you pronounce you will be judged, and with the measure you use it will be measured to you.

In all honesty, the measure *I* want used is a measure that equates to mercy. Maybe you prefer that as well.

When the Bible says mercy triumphs over judgement, it does not mean mercy lets everything go, or that bad things should be excused.

No! Mercy triumphs over judgement, because there is blessing attached if we are merciful.

The definition of mercy that Jesus uses in this passage has deep Hebrew and Aramaic meaning. The word literally means the epitome of sympathy and empathy. Mercy is not the exercise of power. It is the ability to see things with another person's perspective. It means seeing things through their eyes, thinking with their mind, and feeling with their emotion.[6]

Now put that definition of mercy into the framework of the game. As our hands are interlocked in the battle, Jesus' definition of mercy would require me to appreciate and value my opponents' pain. It would be necessary to let my power and strength be under control, to the point that I give mercy *regardless* of my ability to withhold it.

This definition of mercy is the only way we can ever be merciful to an enemy.

Growing up I played sports. If you play sports long enough, you will probably witness a few intense mercy matches. A lot of guys who played sports were strong, and there would always be one guy that was really good at getting the other guys to cry mercy.

I remember one particular match very clearly. There was a guy who continually picked on those he deemed weak.

He always seemed to be pushing someone around – a real bully. There was another guy who was huge but very quiet. He would usually just watch things, and nobody really messed with him because he was so big.

For a while, he just watched the mean bully picking on the others. Eventually he had enough. One day he stood up and challenged the bully to a game. Shortly after they started playing, the bully started yelling, "Mercy! Mercy! Mercy!" That gentle giant of a man did not say a word and just sat back down. He had the power to crush the other guy, but he did not.

*That* is mercy.

This is the deeper meaning of mercy that Jesus wants His disciples to understand. Not only does God give mercy to *them*, but if they will also be merciful with one another, there is blessing attached. That same message is for us as well. If we are merciful, we will experience mercy.

**Challenging Mercy**

Sometimes it is easier to be merciful with a friend, but that is not mercy, that is friendship. What Jesus describes is not natural or ordinary. This mercy is for the one who in our own thinking does not deserve it.

We make a lot of excuses as to why someone does not deserve mercy. Sometimes we say things like, "Look, God, you just don't understand. You don't know what it's like. You don't know what we've experienced." But God took away every excuse when He sent His only son, so He could know every feeling we could have and every temptation we could experience. Jesus was wholly God, and wholly flesh.

Look at Matthew 5:7 again.
*Matthew 5:7*
Blessed are the merciful, for they shall receive mercy.

Through Jesus, God became flesh, and in that, He is able to offer us mercy. In return He pronounces that if we will be merciful with each other, there is blessing for us.

Later in the Bible, Jesus was asked about forgiveness and how many times a person should forgive. In response, Jesus tells a story that draws a greater picture of forgiveness through the parable of the unforgiving servant.

*Matthew 18:21-22*
Then Peter came up and said to him, "Lord, how often will my brother sin against me, and I forgive him? As many as seven times?" Jesus said to him, "I do not say to you seven times, but seventy-seven times.

In other words, Jesus tells Peter to keep going, it is a lot more than seven. Then, Jesus paints a picture of forgiveness by telling a story to illustrate the true intent of His answer.

*Matthew 18:23-24*
"Therefore, the kingdom of heaven may be compared to a king who wished to settle accounts with his servants. When he began to settle, one was brought to him who owed him ten thousand talents."

In modern terms, ten thousand talents is the equivalent of many, many, many, many, years of wages.
*Matthew 18:25-26*

"And since he could not pay, his master ordered him to be sold, with his wife and children and all that he had, and payment to be made. So, the servant fell on his knees, imploring him, 'Have patience with me, and I will pay you everything."

In other words, the servant is begging for mercy.

*Matthew 18:27*
"And out of pity for him, the master of that servant released him and forgave him the debt."

In reality, since the man truly owed this debt, the master had the power to sell him and his family. So, it is remarkable that instead, he shows mercy and forgives a massive debt.

*Matthew 18:28*
"But when that same servant went out, he found one of his fellow servants who owed him a hundred denarii"

One hundred denarii is a minuscule amount compared to what this servant had just been forgiven.

*Matthew 18:29-35*
"and seizing him, he began to choke him, saying, 'Pay what you owe.' So, his fellow servant fell down and pleaded with him, 'Have patience with me, and I will pay you.' He refused and went and put him in prison until he should pay the debt. When his fellow servants saw what had taken place, they were greatly distressed, and they went and reported to their master all that had taken place. Then his master summoned him and said to him, 'You

wicked servant! I forgave you all that debt because you pleaded with me. And should not you have had mercy on your fellow servant, as I had mercy on you?' And in anger his master delivered him to the jailers, until he should pay all his debt. So also my heavenly Father will do to every one of you, if you do not forgive your brother from your heart."

In context, Jesus revealed that if we do not have mercy for one another, God is not going to have mercy on us.

It is not natural to be merciful, because normally we are driven by power, control, and the ability to win. Through the giving of mercy God provides blessing to us, and that changes everything.

**To be merciful defuses my perspective. It calms my interpretation of the situation and makes way for blessing.**

There are many things that hold us back from forgiving or having mercy with someone. Many times, we want what we think we are owed, more than we want to receive God's blessings. We need God to change our perspective by diffusing what we desire through His lens.

Our lens is often selfish. Our perspective is based on what *we* can get out of the situation. We focus on what we are owed and negate everything God has given us.
The story of the unforgiving servant is an example of the root of that mindset.

There can be a lot of emotion tied to difficult

circumstances. It is like wrestlers going at each other. One says, "You let go first, then I'll let go," or "You quit pushing first, then I'll quit pushing." That attitude results in a standoff, and often does not end well.

But if we allow God to diffuse our perspectives and calm us down, it changes the situations. The battle is squashed, because that is what mercy does.

**To be merciful defines my purpose. It calibrates the measure of justice and makes way for blessing.**

Calibration guarantees the measurement being used will produce accurate results. God does not just want to calm us in the situation, He wants to calibrate us to make sure our perspective is correct. He wants us to understand what is truly going on in the situation.

When we tune into the emotion, feelings, reason, and value of the person standing before us, it changes our perception. When we see the other person as God's creation, mercy can do its work, and blessing comes.

**To be merciful deactivates my preference. It conforms me to God's perspective and makes way for blessing.**

In any situation, each person involved has their own idea how things should turn out, but in every circumstance, we have a choice. We can receive a refreshed understanding of God's perfect will, or we can react from our own imperfect preferences.

When God diffuses our perspective, it defines our *purpose*, and deactivates our *preference*.

Think of that person who irritates you, who frustrates you, who has greatly hurt you. Now imagine you are in a mercy match with them, and you have them where you want them. You may have the power to destroy them, but mercy calms, calibrates, and now conforms you to God's will.

**Perhaps you are thinking *that* person does not deserve mercy. I will let you in on a secret – neither do you or I.**

We need the power of the Holy Spirit to calm and calibrate us by deactivating, our preference and conforming us to God's will.

In every situation God, the all-powerful, the one with all authority in Heaven and on Earth, invites us to interlock our hands with His and declare that we need His mercy. In any circumstance we can ask God to exercise His power in and through our lives.

Mercy happens when we ask God to calm us, calibrate us, and conform us to His will.

Jesus needed His disciples to understand this, because when they came off the mountain, there would be situations where their natural tendency would be to crush, take revenge, and grab for control.

He wanted them to know they could trust that His power would be more than enough. We need that, too.

Mercy can only be given where it is not deserved, where it

is not earned, and where it is not leveraged.

Have you ever wronged someone else, and needed mercy? We can all think of situations where someone forgave us. When have you given mercy? It is not a question of whether or not we need to *receive* mercy, because I am telling you, every one of us needs it. It is often easier to identify the times we *need* mercy than the times we need to give mercy.

The understanding of true Biblical mercy was so important that Jesus wanted His closest followers to understand it. So, He drew them to a higher place, away from the masses, to show them there is blessing in being merciful.

## Questions

1. Where do you need to let God defuse your interpretation of a difficult situation?


2. How has your measure of justice been different than God's? How can you allow God to calibrate the scale you use?


3. Where does God need to conform your preference in a situation to His?

# CHAPTER SEVEN – BLESSING IN PURE HEARTS

## Just a Little Impurity

Most of us would say that purity is important. When it comes to water or food, we certainly appreciate it. No one would probably ever say they are okay with dirty water or contaminated food.

We are convinced purity is valuable when it comes to what we ingest. But often, when it comes to spiritual matters, we live contrary to that belief. The things we allow, or do not allow in our lives speak to our understanding of purity.

One of the best illustrations I have heard of purity came from a children's pastor who was doing a series on important life qualities. One of the topics was purity. To demonstrate, a huge pan of brownies was brought in. She served each student a piece and talked about purity as they were enjoying their treat. She said. "Sometimes we allow things in our lives, and we say it's no big deal. Well it is not that big a deal with these brownies either. When I was baking them, there was one little mouse dropping that fell in. But it is okay, because it was just one. It was the same color, so you probably won't even notice it."

Now, as far as I know, there were no real mouse droppings in the brownies. Still, you can imagine the kid's reactions.

What a perfect example of how purity works!

Just like those brownies, we sometimes think a little thing here or there is not a big deal. But, just like a mouse dropping in the brownie batter, it is significant! Sometimes, in the spiritual we do that and then wonder why we have so many issues.

## True Purity

A working definition of purity could be a freedom from *any* corruption, defilement, or contamination.

As Christians, we would probably say that is how we want to live. The thing is, despite our best intentions, we all struggle in this area to some degree. We often allow things in our lives, because we can justify them in our minds. At a spiritual level, it should not be that way. It is not good for us, and when we allow it, there are consequences.

Impurity is a path for sin in our lives, but purity opens up the path to follow God. If we want to see God do a work in our lives, purity is the road we must take. Unfortunately, the enemy knows it, and he will do what he can to deter us.

Even with Adam and Eve, the enemy worked in the area of purity. Right from the beginning, he began to defy and defile what God said.

*Genesis 3:1*
Now the serpent was more crafty than any other beast of the field that the Lord God had made. He said to the

74

woman, "Did God actually say, 'You shall not eat of any tree in the garden'?"

The enemy was trying to get just one little thing in their minds to question the character and motive of God. Not a huge deal, but just a little question to create an impurity in the perfect relationship between the creation and the Creator.

The book of Proverbs offers us a way to safeguard ourselves from impurity.

*Proverbs 4:23-27*
Keep your heart with all vigilance, for from it flow the springs of life.

Purity is about what we allow in. To please God, we must get rid of anything that causes an impurity in our hearts. To be pure in heart means being unaffected by the world, the enemy of our soul, or *anything* that causes us to turn away from God.

In the Sermon on the Mount, Jesus teaches His disciples what it is to be blessed. He has taken them up away from the crowds to have a face-to-face conversation. Each lesson would be critical to them and the experiences they would have when they came down from the mountain.

*Matthew 5:2-7*
And he opened his mouth and taught them, saying:
"Blessed are the poor in spirit, for theirs is the kingdom of heaven.
Blessed are those who mourn, for they shall be comforted.
Blessed are the meek, for they shall inherit the earth.

Blessed are those who hunger and thirst for righteousness, for they shall be satisfied.
Blessed are the merciful, for they shall receive mercy."

And now He teaches them this:

*Matthew 5:8*
Blessed are the pure in heart, for they shall see God.

**Pure in Heart**

Seeing God is a wonderful blessing, and one that all Christians desire. Scripture reveals the reverse as a reality. Those who are not pure in heart are not blessed, and are going to miss God.

**To be blessed understands that our persuasions affect our purity. Persuasions address our influences and inspirations.**

Everyone is influenced by something, and one of the principal persuaders in our lives is our perception of time.

Time itself is not the issue though. It becomes an impurity when it hinders our time with the Lord. We know time with Him is important. Still, it becomes an issue when we do not make our time with Jesus a priority. We busy ourselves with everything else we think has value and excuse away the time we could spend with Him.

Put this in the context of our story. Jesus is going up on the mountain to teach something important. Place yourself as one of the disciples. You know what He has to say is significant, but you think, "I love everything about what is going on, and I want to follow Jesus, but I just don't have time to go up on the mountain with Him right now."

Impurity can take many forms in our lives, but often has roots in those things that influence and inspire us. For example, people sometimes forfeit time with the Lord for sports, hobbies, entertainment, or social media. Others set their relationship with God aside for work, personal fulfillment, financial success, or the pursuit of happiness.

It is not that hobbies, sports, money, or financial security are wrong, but those things can act as impurities if we are not careful. They can influence and drive us. The truth is, by looking at the wrong things, we may be missing out on what we already have.

Paul gives us a great picture of this kind of persuasion in Galatians.

*Galatians 5:7-9*
You were running well. Who hindered you from obeying the truth? This persuasion is not from him who calls you. A little leaven leavens the whole lump.

A small amount of leaven (or yeast) can impact a large batch of dough. It is like having a pan full of brownies with just one little mouse dropping in it. No one would be okay with even a little impurity like that in their food. It is a big deal in what we eat, and it certainly is in our spiritual lives as well.

Our persuasions can influence us away from the things of

God. Not all persuasions are inherently bad, but some are not from God.

Persuasions that distract can come quickly and are often unplanned. It is especially easy to become sidetracked in the heat of the moment. Maybe you were on the right path, growing in your relationship with the Lord. Then something unexpected happened, and your focus turned.

Focusing on what is going on around us, may cause us to think we do not have time to focus on God. Lack of time with Him is commonly excused as no big deal. In truth, it is a *very* big deal. Time with the Lord is essential to guard our hearts from those influences that pull us away from Him. When we get distracted, we need to make a point of refocusing on God in a more purposeful way.

Up on that mountain, away from the crowds, Jesus described what it meant to be pure in spirit and uninfluenced by the persuasions of life. He made it clear that when we recognize and avoid those influences, we are blessed, because then we are going to see God!

**To be blessed understands that our affiliations affect our purity. Affiliations and associations reveal the effects of our connections.**

### Our Affiliates and Associates

Ask yourself these questions.

Who are the people you hang around?

Who has your ear?

Christian or not, we sometimes spend time with individuals we should not. As Christians, however, we usually do so with the best of intention. I have heard people say they consider some not-so-good relationships "mission fields." It sounds like a good idea. The problem is, the people saying that usually are not behaving like missionaries.

What often happens is rather than influencing the person they are with; they end up moving closer and closer to the impurity. It is like living in a funnel.

A good indicator is when we say things like, "I probably shouldn't do this," then do it anyway. When those around us influence us to do the very things we know we should not, it is a sign that we have allowed impurity in. When that happens, we often wonder why the person we are trying to influence is not turning. In fact, what is really happening is that we are the ones being turned.

Our affiliations affect our ability to be pure of heart, and we must guard against that.

Understand, I am not saying you should not hang out with sinners. What I *am* saying is that your relationships have everything to do with your path in life. If your biggest associations are with those who lead you away from the Lord, it is going to show. Those persuasions are going to affect your purity of heart, and *that* is going to affect you.

Just look at what Paul tells the Corinthians.

*1 Corinthians 15:33*
Do not be deceived: "Bad company ruins good morals."

**To be blessed understands that our validations affect our purity. Validations deal with our representations and play out in our demonstrations.**

Persuasions are the things we believe in. Everyone has certain things that persuade them to react, believe, or behave a certain way. Problems arise, though, when the enemy uses what influences us in the places we go for validation.

By nature, humans have a great need for understanding and acceptance. Some people are validated by another's words, and others by accomplishments, degrees, or success. People look for affirmation in countless ways, and we have probably all looked for external validation at some time. As Christians, it becomes troublesome when we look for anything or anyone but God, our Creator, to affirm us.

Validation outside God may temporarily make us feel better, but any source outside Him is not sustainable.

Validation in and through God, comes by understanding who *He* is and who we are in Him. It comes from knowing that we have a savior who loves us, is for us, and is not against us.

Jesus is the source of true validation, because He does not just know what is going on *around* us, He knows what is going on *in* us. He created us, He knows where we are, and has a plan for our lives!

Just as Paul warned the Galatians, we must also watch for those things that may cut in on us. We must guard our hearts and only allow ourselves to be validated by the one who knows us intimately.

**When we understand who He says we are, we have true, lasting, and authentic validation!**

As Christians, we are called to be ambassadors and representatives of the Lord. Perhaps you have heard someone say that Christian's think they are perfect. The truth is, we are Christians because we are *not* perfect. Being a Christian means confessing our need for a savior, because left to ourselves, the best we are ever going to demonstrate is our impurity.

Paul knew the Word, and he knew God. From this understanding, he gives a great example of representations and demonstrations in his first letter to the Corinthians. As a Pharisee of Pharisees, he knew what it meant be religious, but his words express a healthy perspective of himself.

*1 Corinthians 2:1*
And I, when I came to you, brothers, did not come proclaiming to you the testimony of God with lofty speech or wisdom.

Notice, he was not trying to show off, or to impress the Corinthians with how much he knew. He was just trying to tell them *who* he knew.

*1 Corinthians 2:2-5*
For I decided to know nothing among you except Jesus Christ and him crucified. And I was with you in weakness

and in fear and much trembling, and my speech and my message were not in plausible words of wisdom, but in demonstration of the Spirit and of power, so that your faith might not rest in the wisdom of men but in the power of God.

Paul's words demonstrate purity of life. He is stating that our faith does not rest in the wisdom of men, but in the power of God.

The world offers many wonderful things that we can be part of – that is our privilege. Our *right* as Christians is to share with others the good news of the one who died for us, who has a plan for us, who holds the hope, and who holds the future. That is the power of the Holy Spirit through us to the world.

Jesus taught the truth of blessing, because without it, He knew we might miss the true meaning. We could be walking in a blessed state of being and not even know it.

Some time ago, Heather and I redid our deck. The stain was very expensive, and it was painstaking and messy to apply it, but we got it done; however, just after we finished, we realized the forecast said rain was coming.

We were both frustrated and worried. The directions for the stain said it would take twenty-four to forty-eight hours to dry, but the storm was due to in less than ten hours. I remember thinking, "This is not good! Oh, Lord please hold off the rain!"

Well the next day, I woke up early, still not sure what I was going to see outside. I heard it raining and remember feeling disappointed that the Lord did not hold back the rain like I had prayed. I was irritated because we worked really hard on the project. All I could think was that it was going to look like junk because of the rain. When I looked out the window, it was clear the rain had not done anything to the deck. Nothing had been ruined, and it still looked great. In that moment, I realized, the Lord did not need to hold off the rain, even though that had been *my* solution.

Why did I question God? Even if the deck had been ruined, I would have gotten over it. Deck staining may not seem like a big deal, but how I handled it is a great example of impurity. My perspective had allowed disappointment to creep in and could have potentially created a wedge between me and the Lord.

Rather than focusing on our own agendas, we need to realize that God knows what is going on, and what is needed. In every circumstance, we need to thank Him, because whatever He does is good.

When we can understand and do that, we are blessed!

In another scripture the Psalmist writes about the idea of means, motives, and the manner by which we approach God by faith.

*Psalm 24:4-5*
He who has clean hands and a pure heart,
    who does not lift up his soul to what is false
    and does not swear deceitfully.
He will receive blessing from the Lord
    and righteousness from the God of his salvation.

Let me break this down for you.

"*He who has Clean Hands*" refers to the **means**. It is what we do and do not do from a physical and spiritual principle.

He who has "*a Pure Heart*" speaks to our **motives**. It is the *why* behind what we do.

Both the *means* and the *motives* are part of the purity that God wants to work out in our lives. And when it says "*does not lift up his soul to what is false, and does not swear deceitfully,*" it refers to the **manner** by which we do things through our character and integrity.

M*otives* justify the *means*, and not always in a good way. But the Holy Spirit empowers us in those moments and helps us in the manner by which we do things. He is the one who works through us on behalf of the Lord so we can be ambassadors and representatives.

Look at our working definition of purity one more time. It is the freedom from *any* corruption, defilement, or contamination.

One lie, one action, one infraction, one secret sin… We can excuse it and say it is not really that big of a deal. It was just one little thing in the brownies, right?

What is that thing you just keep pushing around? Where has your life started to blend into the negative influences in your life?

On the mountain, Jesus is talking to the people who are going to share the Gospel going forward. Very difficult times and incredible persecutions would be in store for them. He was telling them they are blessed, because if they stay pure in heart, they will see God.

Later in scripture, Jesus declares He is the way, the truth, and the life, and that no one can come to the Father except through Him. Knowing that, we must apply *His* words, and *His* understanding to His teaching.

Read the scripture again.

*Matthew 5:8*
Blessed are the pure in heart, for they shall see God.

The blessing for those who are pure in heart is that they get to see God! What an awesome message for us all!

## Questions

1. Where have you allowed wrong influences to affect your purity?


2. How have the people you associate with affected your purity?


3. Where have validations that are not from God affected your purity?


4. Where have you held the line and turned your heart to the things of God?

# CHAPTER EIGHT – BLESSING AS PEACEMAKERS

## Peacemakers Defined

Jesus took His closest followers up the mountain to share deep spiritual revelations with them. He disclosed the certainty of blessing when they are poor in spirit, mournful, and meek. He revealed the available blessings when they hunger and thirst for righteousness, and He tells them there is blessing when they are merciful and pure in heart. Now, He begins to reveal the blessing for peacemakers.

*Matthew 5:9*
"Blessed are the peacemakers, for they shall be called sons of God."

It is critical that we understand who peacemakers are and what they do, because Jesus says there is blessing attached to making peace. He says those that do make peace will be called children of God.

If I asked what it means to be a peacemaker, you might say it is someone who is timid, friendly, cooperative, adaptable, easy-going, or empathetic. You might even define peacemakers as individuals who solve problems.

When asked what they *do*, most of us would say that peacemakers make peace.

When we look at peacemakers in a spiritual sense, the definition is quite different than what we may naturally think.

**What Peacemaking is Not**

**To be blessed, peacemakers are defined by their source of peace and should not be confused with being peacekeepers.**

As Christians, we are ambassadors and representatives of the Gospel message. Our calling brings peace into situations.

The peacemakers Jesus talks about should not be confused with peacekeepers. Making peace is very different from keeping it. Jesus' brother, James, gives us insight into the difference between the two.

*James 3:17-18*
But the wisdom from above is first pure, then peaceable, gentle, open to reason, full of mercy and good fruits, impartial and sincere. And a harvest of righteousness is sown in peace by those who make peace.

James says a *harvest* of peace is sown by those who make peace. Harvest only happens when something is planted. Farmers sow seeds in anticipation of reaping a harvest. In the framework of Jesus words, the message is speaking of sowing seeds of *peace*.

Unlike farmers whose harvest is often impacted by external elements, peacemakers harvest peace *regardless* of another person's response or non-response. This is big! Just as the disciples, *we* must understand this in a deep, personal way.

*As followers of Christ, we are called to be peacemakers.*

However, peace does mean the non-existence of distress or difficulty. It does not imply there will never be struggle. Jesus is not saying we are peacemakers as long as there is no conflict.

Sometimes we struggle with that. Jesus' followers would have understood the word from the context of the Hebrew language. Their understanding of the word "peace" included everything that makes or provides for a person's highest good, *regardless* of the situation.[7]

Jesus is using the word in *that* framework. He is telling His disciples that peace is available no matter what the circumstances are. Peace is not determined by what is going on, or if the situation ever changes. No matter what condition we find ourselves in, we *can* make peace as a peacemaker.

In difficult circumstances, we are promised blessing as peacemakers. The good news is that the ability to make and experience peace does not rest on *our* shoulders. Walking as peacemakers into the middle of the valley of the shadow of death is beyond human strength.

But we do not walk alone. God promises to be with us in those times.

*Psalm 23:4*
Even though I walk through the valley of the shadow of death, I will fear no evil, for you are with me; your rod and your staff, they comfort me.

The Psalmist is saying that *whatever* we go through, and whatever the circumstances, peace is available. We do not and cannot accomplish that peace in our own power. It comes from and through Jesus, the Shepherd. It is His power that works in and through us as a peacemaker.

Peacekeepers do not have the same ability or access that peacemakers do. We are called to make peace in difficult situations and to create opportunities to bring about civility, respect, love, and ultimately balance.

**To be blessed, peacemakers are determined by their motives and should not be confused with being peace loving.**

To be clear, it is not that peacemakers do not love peace – they do. There is a subtle difference between the two in what motivates them.

If you have young children at home, you probably know what it is to want peace. Often as parents, we will do whatever is necessary to make that happen. Let them watch the show a little longer, stay up a little later, play a little louder and so on. In our minds and in the moment, the compromise is worth the peace.

That is being a peacekeeper. Wanting peace is not a bad thing, but peacemakers do not just *want* peace, they *make* peace!

Many people avoid conflict because they love peace. They allow threatening or dangerous circumstances to advance under the misconception they are keeping the peace. There is a belief that avoidance fosters peace. In reality, it mounds trouble in the future, because avoiding action just puts off the unavoidable.

Some people passively accept difficult situations, because they are afraid of the trouble that may result. But often peace is found through the struggle when we actively face things. Biblical, blessed-peace does not come through dodging issues that must be dealt with. It comes from facing them head on, dealing with them, and overcoming them in the strength of Jesus.

We are called to be peacemakers. In the context of what Jesus is talking about, there is blessing attached, because peacemakers are known as children of God. The same is not true for keepers of the peace.

Peacemakers make peace in even the most difficult situations. They do not do that through passive acceptance of the circumstances or because they are afraid of trouble. Peacemaking requires actively facing matters in faith through Jesus.

As His children, we make peace *in* and *through* Him. No one can do that in and of themselves.
For *that* reason, we are blessed.

**To be blessed, peacemakers are designated by their position and should not be confused with being peace mediators.**

In the framework of sporting events, referees are mediators. They preside over the game as the authority and stand between opposing sides to make on-the-fly decisions that enforce specific guidelines and rulings.

Often referees bring everyone together to make sure each side understands and follows the rules.

Sometimes when conflicts arise, it is almost as though we put on black and white striped shirts and become referees. This is especially true when we insert ourselves into situations which we were not designed to be involved. Jesus did not tell the disciples to be referees; He called them to be peacemakers, and the peace we bring only comes *through* Him.

The blessing Jesus describes is spiritual. His anointing makes us peacemakers.

Too many people go into areas they were never designed to go, and that is the worst place to be. We must make sure we always go in under *His* anointing when we go into any conflict, because there can be no solution without Him. We make peace as His child and representative, so He must be in the forefront.

In his first letter to his disciple Timothy, Paul explains what our position should be when it comes to mediation.

*1 Timothy 2:5*
For there is one God, and there is one mediator between God and men, the man Christ Jesus.

Paul is clear. Christ alone is the mediator. You and I are neither equipped, nor appointed to be the solution. Peace only comes by bringing Jesus into the situation.

In the physical world, we understand the concept of authority. If our kids tell us a story about a problem on the playground, we ask if they told the teacher, because the right solution is to tell the person in charge. In the spiritual, the same truth applies. In tough situations, we must bring in the One who owns the battle.

*1 Samuel 17:47*
For the battle is the Lord's.

Peacemakers go into conflicts as representatives of Jesus. In any situation, we not only represent Him, but carry His authority. We bring His solutions, His love, His power, His truth, and His Word.

The book of Isaiah in the Old Testament was written hundreds of years before Christ came on the scene. His words prophetically spoke of the birth of Jesus and proclaim that he is the Prince of Peace.

*Isaiah 9:6*
For to us a child is born,
    to us a son is given;
and the government shall be upon his shoulder,
    and his name shall be called

Wonderful Counselor, Mighty God,
   Everlasting Father, Prince of Peace.

As Christians, we are ordained to be peacemakers in and
through Him, but when there is conflict, we need Jesus in
the middle. When we enter a situation, the presence of the
Holy Spirit in us brings the Prince of Peace, Mighty God,
Everlasting Father, and Wonderful Counselor to the table.

*Romans 8:14*
For all who are led by the Spirit of God are sons of God.

No situation is beyond peace, but *every* situation is in need
of a peacemaker. We are peacemakers in and through
Jesus, and just like Jewish rabbis, our highest
achievement should be to attain right relationship with
people.

Away from the frenzy of the crowd, up on the mountain,
that is the message Jesus is teaching those who are
closest to Him. They needed to understand it, and we do
too.

As Jesus spoke to His closest followers, His message
unfolded a true meaning of the blessing and power of a
peacemaker; they will be called sons of God.

It does not matter how smart we are or if we can create
solutions or solve problems. When we are led by His Spirit,
our identity is as children of God.

Peacemakers bring assurance and balance because of
who they represent. They do not represent what they *think*

the solution is. They represent the King of Kings and Lord of Lords, and *that* is a foundation we can firmly stand on.

## Troublemakers and Peacemakers

Often times troublemakers and peacemakers run in the same circle. It stands to reason that as believers we *will* find ourselves in challenging circumstances. What gets us into trouble is thinking we can fix things on our own. Without the Lord's anointing, we just create more trouble. God wants us aligned with Him as peacemakers.

Throughout my life, there have been specific people I call when there is trouble. These individuals are the ones I want in the middle of any difficult situation because they are peacemakers. They may or may not have the words or wisdom to fix the issue, but they bring the Lord's presence into every circumstance.

That is what God called His Church to be.

Jesus thought that was important enough to talk to His disciples about in His first sermon to them. He wanted them to understand that He was the one empowering them as His children to go into any situation as peacemakers.

What was true, and available to them on the mountain, is true and available to us today. The blessing is that we go in His anointing under His authority.

In any situation, the Lord is there to help us accomplish His work, and to give us His power, His wisdom, and His anointing. We can invite Him into any battle, whether in our families, marriages, friendships, or places of work.

Just as John says in his Epistle:

*John 1:5*
The light shines in the darkness, and the darkness has not overcome it.

The big question is what areas of your life need peace? The answer lies in this statement:

Where we actively make peace through Jesus, His blessing and anointing reside.

## Questions

1. What is the difference between peacemakers and peacekeepers? Why does keeping the peace fail long term?


2. Where have you avoided taking action for the sake of peace? How did that resolve (or not resolve) the situation?


3. How does being a peacemaker differ from being a peace mediator? Why is it dangerous to go into situations you are not anointed for?

# CHAPTER NINE – BLESSING WHEN PERSECUTED

## The Meaning of Blessing

The setting of the Beatitudes is intimate. His closest disciples have left the crowds and followed Jesus up a mountain. In that higher, more remote place, He leads them through a series of statements, teachings, and stories about what it means to be blessed.

Every point of the sermon brought them to a deeper understanding of a relationship with Him.

As He presented these truths, the next blessing He shares is more challenging for them. Jesus taught them about blessings that encompassed the difficulties of applying His truths. Now, the disciples were going to have to lean into Him in order to fully realize the message that there is blessing in persecution for righteousness sake.

If we put ourselves into their place, we can probably relate to how they may have felt. Sometimes the things of the Lord are difficult and beyond our comprehension, and they definitely challenge our sense of comfort.

However, many times the messages that are *most* uncomfortable are the ones we need to understand the most. What Jesus was about to share would be hard, but they needed it, and we do too.

Life is difficult whether we are Christians or not, but without Jesus it is impossible. He was about to unfold that there would always be a choice to do life on their own or with Him. With Jesus there was blessing available. That blessing is beyond circumstances, feelings, or emotions.

The blessing Jesus describes is available even in the midst of difficulty and persecution.

*Matthew 5:10*
"Blessed are those who are persecuted for righteousness' sake, for theirs is the kingdom of heaven."

**Persecuted for Righteousness' Sake**

It seems reasonable that when someone does something wrong, they get in trouble or experience discipline or consequences. We can rationalize if someone is hated or disliked when they have done something to deserve it from a rationality standpoint. However, it makes no sense to us when someone is persecuted and there has been no crime, no slight, no misstep, no wrong done.

This is exactly what Jesus is teaching His disciples. He is telling them they are blessed when they do the right thing and are mistreated anyway.

He is saying that when they are persecuted, despite doing

what is correct according to God, they are blessed. Jesus wanted them to grasp this. It is a radical statement, but they needed to understand it and we must too.

Paul the Apostle wrote much of the New Testament of the Bible. In a letter to his follower Timothy, he explains this:

*2 Timothy 3:12*
Indeed, all who desire to live a godly life in Christ Jesus will be persecuted.

Paul's letter to Timothy is straightforward and clear, if you live for Jesus you *will* be persecuted!

A statement like that may make you wonder why anyone would want to live for Jesus. We typically do not sign up for things that bring us trouble. Life brings difficulties with or without Jesus, but the blessing we have with Jesus far outweighs the hardships without Him. Jesus said that even if there is persecution for the sake of righteousness, we are blessed!

With Him, even when the journey is difficult, there is good news. The truth is, choosing an alternative to His ways has a payout, but *the end result is not good.*

What makes Jesus' teaching difficult for some is that He is not referring to every mistreatment. He has added a definitive in the blessing, and it qualifies the type of persecution that is blessed.

Read the scripture again.

*Matthew 5:10*
"Blessed are those who are persecuted for righteousness' sake, for theirs is the kingdom of heaven."
Understand, this righteousness has nothing to do with our own morality or goodness. The Bible describes our righteousness; the good we think we have, like this:

*Isaiah 64:6*
All of us have become like one who is unclean, and all our righteous acts are like a polluted garment. We all fade like a leaf, and our iniquities, like the wind, take us away.

Biblical righteousness means right standing with God. And that only comes through the atoning work of His Son Jesus Christ. The implication of the blessing qualifier is that the blessing is for those who follow and obey Him.

Jesus closest disciples had to understand this. They were the ones who would take the Gospel message and move it forward for all generations. Jesus wanted them to know there is blessing even when people hated them for doing the right thing.

Following Jesus encompasses every area of our lives, so there is potential for persecution in every area as well. Still, our relationship to Him requires obedience and faithfulness in everything involving our lives.

As followers of Jesus, it is conceivable that our obedience would unravel our social life, unsettle our home life, and upset our work life.

That message was true on the mountain and is true today.

Following Jesus has the possibility to upset our lives in the natural flow of things.

**To be blessed when persecuted "for righteousness' sake," there is a reception versus participation situation that exposes our willingness to partake.**

We have all heard the saying, "It is better to give than receive." It is a nice sentiment, but if we are honest, we would admit that we all like to receive things. We want to receive when it comes to what God has for us. Hopefully we want *everything* He offers.

It is likely you are familiar with the concept of a reception. Oftentimes people have wedding receptions where the bride and groom are given gifts. At that reception, there is an element of participation. The bride and groom are expected to take part in the celebration. It would be odd for them to skip the reception and still expect to receive gifts.

What Jesus offers is not just to be received. There is an expectation of participation. Yet somehow in modern Christianity we sometimes want to receive what He offers without participation.

Put that in the context of communion. When we participate in communion, we celebrate what Jesus did and thank Him for what He has given us. We are participating in His crucifixion by remembering what He has done.

Take a look at what Paul tells the Corinthians in his letter to them:

*1 Corinthians 10:16*
The cup of blessing that we bless, is it not a participation in the blood of Christ? The bread that we break, is it not a participation in the body of Christ?
In communion we participate, we do not just receive.

Sometimes people claim to be followers of Jesus, but live according to their own feelings and desire. Then when the consequences of their choices happen, they call it persecution. They are likely confusing true persecution with the cost of their actions. That is what Jesus is showing His disciples. He is not saying that just because bad times come, they are blessed. He adds the qualifier, *"for righteousness sake."*

A relationship with Christ requires more than just saying you are a follower; it involves action and faith for the blessing to take root. Sometimes, people claim to be followers of Christ, but their lives do not reflect it.

We cannot just say we follow; we must actually follow. Look what Jesus' brother James says about participation.

*James 1:22-25*
But be doers of the word, and not hearers only, deceiving yourselves. For if anyone is a hearer of the word and not a doer, he is like a man who looks intently at his natural face in a mirror. For he looks at himself and goes away and at once forgets what he was like. But the one who looks into the perfect law, the law of liberty, and perseveres, being no hearer who forgets but a doer who acts, he will be blessed in his doing.

Jesus told His closest followers that this journey would be very hard, but His message was clear. When they are persecuted for righteousness sake, there is an expectation of a spiritual return, and that is a blessing, because their blessing in this instance is the Kingdom of Heaven.

**To be blessed when persecuted "for righteousness' sake," there is a voluntary versus compulsory condition that discloses the expectation of spiritual return.**

Jesus often illustrated spiritual concepts through stories. One was about three servants whose master had entrusted each of them with a valuable monetary investment of a talent. The master leaves for a time, but when he returns, he finds the first two not only used their talent but invested what he gave them. They returned it to him with interest; however, the third servant buried the talent, and so wasted the return for what he was given.

Take a look at how the master responds.

*Matthew 25:26-30*
But his master answered him, 'You wicked and slothful servant! You knew that I reap where I have not sown and gather where I scattered no seed? Then you ought to have invested my money with the bankers, and at my coming I should have received what was my own with interest. So take the talent from him and give it to him who has the ten talents. For to everyone who has will more be given, and he will have an abundance. But from the one who has not, even what he has will be taken away. And cast the worthless servant into the outer darkness. In that place

103

there will be weeping and gnashing of teeth.'
God does not give without expecting something in return.
He blesses us in many ways, and there is an expectation
of a spiritual return. The servant was disqualified from the
blessing. He missed the requirement to participate.

The master in the story had anticipation of return on what
he gave. Participation in what God offers is voluntary, but
receiving the blessing requires it.

Most of us have probably volunteered at some point or
another. Volunteerism is sometimes viewed differently than
a paid position. When people do not feel obligated, then
sometimes when something better comes along, they do
not show up even though they have committed to
volunteer.

We have to be careful not to treat our walk with Jesus that
way. When something is compulsory, it is required,
obligatory, or mandated by something that steers us. We
cannot serve the Lord based on our feelings or desires.
Following Jesus is not voluntary; it is compulsory.

**Compulsory Christianity**

History reveals the torture that early Christians endured.
Torturous acts were performed on Christians because of
their belief in Jesus. Some were thrown to the lions' dens,
and others were burned to death.

The Emperor Nero dipped Christians in wax, impaled them
on poles around his palace, and ignited them to be used
as living torches to light up his gardens.

Persecution of the early church was common and terrible. However, one of the most common ways which Christians were wronged was on that of the political platform.

At the time of the early church, the Roman Empire included most of the known world.

A unifying principle was created, and the worship of one god was seen as the glue needed to hold society together. Because of that, the government instituted mandatory worship of the spirit of Rome through the goddess Roma.

The citizens of Rome were willing to sacrifice, because Rome had brought peace, solid government, civil order, justice, better roads, and safer seas. There was an element of social respect, so the general public saw this as a good thing. In this worship and spiritual edict, a line was created because early Christians knew there was only one true God.[8]

*John 17:3*
And this is eternal life, that they know you, the only true God, and Jesus Christ whom you have sent.

The government mandate challenged early Christian beliefs, and because of their unwillingness to participate in the worship of the goddess Roma, many were horribly persecuted.

The early church did not live as though their beliefs were voluntary. They lived their faith as compulsory, and because of that, they were blessed. Christianity requires complete devotion to Jesus Christ. When we are completely devoted to Him, His ways may collide with society's ways.

That is the message Jesus was giving His disciples, and it is one we need to understand as well.

### Today's Faith

Even today, there are many things in our culture that chip away at the foundation of the Church. Whether it be sports, civic events, hobbies, or even employment, decisions are often made based on the acceptance of the social norm rather than on the precepts of what it means to be a follower of Jesus. Understand that these things are not always bad in and of themselves. The caution is that they *can* undermine Christian standards.

The solution is to keep the understanding of the blessing qualifier, "*righteousness' sake*," and make decisions from that perspective.

**To be blessed when persecuted "for righteousness' sake," there is a conforming versus transforming position that provides the foundation for our certainty.**

Another societal requirement the early church faced was the yearly requirement to honor Caesar. The Roman government eventually moved from the worship of the goddess Roma, to the worship of the Emperor Caesar. They were required to take a pinch of incense and burn it to Caesar while publicly saying he was lord.

Christian or not, everyone in Rome was expected to

participate. The belief was that citizens would wholly support the government. If they did not, bad things happened. The edict stated that once a citizen burned the incense and declared Caesar as Lord, they were given a certificate. Only *then* were they free to do business and worship where and who they wanted.

Christians found themselves in the middle of a societal ruling and again faced following their beliefs or the crowds. On the surface, what was being asked could have been passed off as good for society, beneficial for the people, and necessary for the government.

It might have seemed excusable, but it went against their core beliefs. For them, there was no choice but to refuse. Christ was Lord, and they would not give the title to anyone but Him.[10]

Calling good evil and evil good is a subtle deception. We have an enemy who wants to steal, kill, and destroy, and he often works in the subtle arena of good and evil. He tries to bring an appearance of balance between what seems good and what seems evil, and it requires Christians to declare a position.

What would our response be if asked to do the same as the early Christians? Would we be willing to refuse, no matter the financial, personal, or physical cost? Would we be able to say *no* and trust the Lord for the outcome?

That is the context of what Jesus was saying to His closest followers up on the mountain. Away from the crowds, He had their attention.

These individuals were going to experience persecution for *"righteousness' sake."* He needed to give them a foundation to work out their faith and understand that they were blessed no matter what.

He started by telling them blessed are the poor in spirit, because theirs is the kingdom of heaven. In each of the next six lessons He continues to teach them deeper revelations of blessing, and each one requires more understanding, more faith, and more reliance on Him.

The lesson on persecution is extremely difficult, but if they grasped the understanding of the first blessing, they would have a firm foundation for this one. The end result is the same blessing as the first; no matter what, they are still blessed and theirs is the Kingdom of Heaven.

The Apostle Paul wrote to those living in Rome, because they were encountering persecution as they lived for Jesus. Here is what he says to them:

*Romans 12:1-2*
I appeal to you therefore, brothers, by the mercies of God, to present your bodies as a living sacrifice, holy and acceptable to God, which is your spiritual worship. Do not be conformed to this world, but be transformed by the renewal of your mind, that by testing you may discern what is the will of God, what is good and acceptable and perfect.

## Questions

1.  Where have you compromised your faith rather than participate in a faith challenging moment?

2. Where have you viewed your Christian journey as voluntary versus compulsory?

3. In what ways has your faith transformed your daily life? If it has not, why?

# CHAPTER TEN – BLESSING WHEN REVILED

## Mountain Training

In the Sermon on the Mount, Jesus trained the disciples for what they would face as His followers. This sermon provides everything Jesus' followers then and now would need for the journey.

What He does is not unlike parenting. In our culture, we may not see it that way. In recent years, our understanding of parenting or training our children has shifted.

The Bible speaks of the importance of training children.

*Proverbs 22:6*
Train up a child in the way he should go; even when he is old, he will not depart from it.

The emphasis in this scripture is on *training* the child, not removing the obstacles. It is not about making the way easy. It is about preparation. Many times, in modern parenting, obstacles are removed.

The child is not being prepared for the way; the way is being prepared for the child. This produces weakness in

111

trials, difficulties, and hard times. Unfortunately, that mindset has bled over into Christianity.

People often think when they become a Christian there will be no problems. A relationship with Christ does not mean things will always go our way, and because we do not understand this, we struggle with the real meaning of blessing.

There on the mountain, Jesus was preparing His disciples for the reality of their journey. He knew it was going to be difficult and dangerous. He explained what will come so that when the difficulties came, they would know they were still blessed. Therefore, the blessing was not contingent on the situation.

Through the Sermon on the Mount, Jesus teaches what it means to be blessed, but why would there be blessing from God if they experienced persecution on His behalf?

Reread this passage:

*Matthew 5:1-10*
Seeing the crowds, he went up on the mountain, and when he sat down, his disciples came to him.
And he opened his mouth and taught them, saying:
"Blessed are the poor in spirit, for theirs is the kingdom of heaven.
Blessed are those who mourn, for they shall be comforted.
Blessed are the meek, for they shall inherit the earth.
Blessed are those who hunger and thirst for righteousness, for they shall be satisfied.
Blessed are the merciful, for they shall receive mercy.

Blessed are the pure in heart, for they shall see God. Blessed are the peacemakers, for they shall be called sons of God."

Each lesson builds on the next. Each describes true blessing. Then finally Jesus says…

Matthew 5:11-12
"Blessed are you when others revile you and persecute you and utter all kinds of evil against you falsely on my account. Rejoice and be glad, for your reward is great in heaven, for so they persecuted the prophets who were before you."

Jesus, the One who later in scripture is declared as the way, the truth, and the life, is speaking this into their lives to prepare them. He does not shield them or water down the message. He does not imply that although hard times come, they will be happy. No! His message is clear. He wants them to understand they are blessed even when difficulty, hardship, and persecution occur.

He is telling them, that in every circumstance there is blessing.

**The Requirements**

**To be blessed in difficulties requires loyalty. It reveals a willingness for faithfulness.**

The disciples had to ask themselves whether or not they wanted to be or not to be with Jesus on the mountain. Going up the mountain required them to move from where they were to follow where Jesus was taking them. They were familiar with the place they had come from.

Perhaps they were even comfortable. Now they were faced with the decision to leave what they knew to follow Him higher up.

In context of our own faith journeys, we all must answer that same question, but to do so requires loyalty.

On the mountain, Jesus told them there was blessing even when they were reviled on His account. That is a difficult thing. The word *reviled* is strong. It means hated, loathed, detested. No matter what came their way, the disciples would have to remain loyal.

Jesus tells His closest followers there is blessing in the difficulty, even the persecution. He says that in the midst of their faith battle, at the heart and soul level, it would require loyalty. They must hold true through integrity with God, and that would necessitate their consistency in every instance.

Sometimes we are not very consistent in our faith. We might be unwavering on the weekend, but when Monday morning comes, we look like completely different people. On the weekend we look like people who love Jesus, but on Monday morning, He is nowhere to be found.

Away from the crowds, Jesus was getting personal with the disciples. He wanted them to understand the importance of loyalty. He wanted them to see that in every difficulty, they were blessed, and so are you!

Jesus wants the true meaning of blessing to go deep into the hearts and minds of His closest followers, and He wants that for you too!

**Understand, loyalty is only tested on the road to difficulty.**

Think about it. It is one thing to say you are loyal to a best friend, spouse, relative, or close childhood friend who has been with you for a long time. However, loyalty is tested when the road gets difficult or problems come. Loyalty dies on the altar of fear, faithlessness, and selfishness.

Jesus is telling the disciples that even when they are persecuted there is a payoff, because they are blessed. They needed to understand that if they hold tight and hold true, there is a Heavenly reward because they are blessed.

**To be blessed in hardship reveals confidence. It requires us to stand firm in the immediate through God.**

**Faithful and Firm**

In troubling times, people often look for areas of strength, confidence, and hope in their lives other than to Jesus. Without the perspective that Jesus gives, we become selfish, think we deserve more than what we are getting, or believe we do not deserve the current situation. Often, we begin to question God.

*The test of confidence comes with unwavering endurance when it values living right more than being liked, despite the circumstance.*

God must be the source of our confidence, and in that we are to stand strong in the immediate through Him.

We can have great confidence in things that ultimately do not matter. We count on relationships, but what happens when the relationship changes? We have assurance because our parents or grandparents are praying for us. What happens when they are gone? Our hope cannot be based on a pastor or someone we highly respect. We cannot place our confidence in anyone but God.

When we put our confidence anywhere else, we miss the power that is available to us.

*Hebrews 10:23*
Let us hold fast the confession of our hope without wavering, for he who promised is faithful.

*Hebrews 10:35-36*
Therefore, do not throw away your confidence, which has a great reward. For you have need of endurance, so that when you have done the will of God you may receive what is promised.

These verses tell us to have confidence in hope, because He is faithful. This kind of confidence is humanly impossible without Jesus. It is easy to talk a good talk, but the testing begins when difficulties happen, when the road seems to have disappeared.

That is where confidence is tested. Whatever the situation, the source of our confidence must be Jesus Christ.

*2 Corinthians 3:4*
Such is the confidence that we have through Christ toward God.

That is what Jesus is telling His disciples on the side of that mountain. Away from the masses, in that higher place, He tells them that when everybody has left them and they feel all alone, they are still blessed!

He is preparing the disciples for what they are going to encounter. He is telling them there is going to be a difficult and challenging road ahead. Even in those times, where they struggle to find the way, they are blessed.

Do not confuse confidence with arrogance, though. The blessing Jesus speaks of is not based on self-esteem, and it does not come through mental or physical strength.

There are times we believe we control the outcome. We think if we are more intentional, speak more positively, become healthier mentally or physically, our situations will change. We convince ourselves we just need to develop better habits.

Making positive changes is not a bad thing, but if what we are trying to accomplish is taking the place of Jesus as the way, the truth, and the life, it is wrong. Ultimately, unless our confidence comes through Him, our solutions are temporary at best.

Other times, we make our confidence situational. We believe our relationship with Jesus would be better if our marriage was better, we had more friends, or we knew the right people.

When Jesus is our source, we are blessed regardless of who or what is around us.

We must place our confidence in Him first, because unless He is our source of strength, we are not going to get any stronger. We have to be faithful and firm in our faith, even in our weakness.

*2 Corinthians 12:10*
For the sake of Christ, then, I am content with weaknesses, insults, hardships, persecutions, and calamities. For when I am weak, then I am strong.

What Christ was saying on the mountain to His disciples was when they were weak, they were blessed. He wanted them to know He would be there and prepare the way.

The blessing comes when confidence is in and through Christ alone!

**To be blessed in oppression remembers honor. It exposes the need for gratitude.**

**The Inerrancy of God**

God is without error or fault. Inerrancy means He is perfect, without blemish, and does not make mistakes.

*2 Samuel 22:31*
This God—his way is perfect; the word of the Lord proves true; he is a shield for all those who take refuge in him.

*Deuteronomy 32:3-4*
For I will proclaim the name of the Lord;
    ascribe greatness to our God!
"The Rock, his work is perfect,
    for all his ways are justice.
God of faithfulness and without iniquity,
    just and upright is he.

Still, when something happens, how many of us have said, "Why would God allow that?" Maybe we have not said it out loud, but if we are honest, many of us have thought it, especially when we feel oppressed.

But God does not fail! He cannot. He will not. He will not mess up, but He is willing to work through our mess-ups. If we are breathing, we are probably a testimony of some major mess-ups! He is perfect and willing to work with us beyond our mistakes, and we should honor Him because of that.

**Reality: Regardless of how oppressed our journey, deep our hurt, terrible, or unfair our situation, He is worthy not only to be praised but to be thanked.**

*Proverbs 3:5*
Trust in the Lord with all your heart,
    and do not lean on your own understanding.

**We do not *just* trust Him in the things we understand or that make sense to us; we trust Him in *all things*!**

*Proverbs 3:6*
In all your ways acknowledge him,
    and he will make straight your paths.

*Honor Him no matter what.*

Jesus was teaching His closest followers that there was the opportunity for blessings in any scenario, no matter what happens. He was telling them even if "*others revile you and persecute you and utter all kinds of evil against you falsely on my account,*" they were blessed, and so are we. We should thank Him and honor Him because of this great blessing.

**Rejoice and Be Glad**

The message in The Beatitudes is that we are blessed regardless of the circumstance, but in verse twelve, Jesus tells them to rejoice and be glad.

*Matthew 5:12*
Rejoice and be glad, for your reward is great in heaven, for so they persecuted the prophets who were before you.

Jesus refers to the persecution that the Old Testament prophets faced. God spoke through them to bring words of correction to His people, and every one of them was persecuted.

Their persecution was not because they said or did wrong things. These individuals were persecuted because they said and did what God told them.

Jesus told His disciples that the reward for any things they endured through hardships or persecutions for His sake would not compare to what they had to look forward to in Him. He was saying the fulfillment of the blessed promise far outweighed any problem they would ever encounter.

The great news; this blessing applies to us too!

He told them to rejoice in that promise! But He does not just want lip service from His followers. He told them to praise and sing out, and be glad about it!

On the side of that mountain, Jesus tried to get through to the heart of His disciples. He wanted them to know there would be hard times, and it would be difficult.

He knew they would want to stop. He knew they were going to want to take matters into their own hands. He knew people were going to hate them because of their relationship with Him. People would actually revile them on account of their testimony, but they needed to know that even in all of that, they were blessed.

To be or not to be faithful in loyalty, in confidence, and in honor to Jesus, we must understand:

- Loyalty means faithfulness and a willingness to hold true and stand firm.

- Confidence is the belief that we can rely on and firmly trust Him.
- Honor is giving respect and gratitude.

Loyalty, confidence, and honor are three words that represent the hallmark of faith that the disciples would need for the journey ahead of them.

Jesus knew they would be killed for their faith. He knew what was coming, but He wanted them to know that through everything that was about to happen, the blessing was theirs.

That same blessing is available to you today, no matter the problem, no matter the heartache. In trouble or persecution, you are blessed!

## Questions

1. Where has concern over potential persecution caused you to be disloyal?


2. Where have you gone for confidence outside of God?


3. How have you failed, or honored God in various situations?

# CONCLUSION

No doubt, there is blessing in knowing the Lord! To experience the blessing, we must take hold of the promises in His Scriptures.

The truths found in the Beatitudes within the Sermon on the Mount reveal what it means to be blessed.

**They contain everything needed for the Christian journey.**

Even though Jesus' message was directed to His closest followers, their truths and applications are for your benefit today.

Just like the disciples, we will experience challenges, difficulties, and heartbreak. We may or may not suffer martyrdom as they did. We may or may not experience loss. There will be moments that test our faith, and we will know, as a follower of Jesus that we must be peacemakers, merciful, and meek.

Every possible human experience finds itself in this mountainside sermon, and it provides the understanding of blessing through Jesus in anything we may encounter.

Though this message is challenging, it is critical, just as it was for Jesus' closest followers. The Church needs this message of blessing to encourage, build up, and prepare for the journey of taking the Gospel of Jesus Christ to the world.

Jesus' mountain message requires us to leave the crowds, the happenings, and the common elements of life. His message requires us to go to an intimate place with Him.

The road may be challenging, but there is a most amazing payoff of reward and blessing!

What God has in store for us far exceeds anything here on earth. Just like the disciples, Jesus tells us to hold true, stand strong, and give thanks, because the best is yet to come!

Church, the message Jesus spoke on the side of the mountain, He speaks to you! The blessing He spoke of on the side of the mountain is available to you today!

*Matthew 5:1-12*
Seeing the crowds, he went up on the mountain, and when he sat down, his disciples came to him. And he opened his mouth and taught them, saying:

"Blessed are the poor in spirit, for theirs is the kingdom of heaven.

Blessed are those who mourn, for they shall be comforted.

Blessed are the meek, for they shall inherit the earth.

Blessed are those who hunger and thirst for righteousness, for they shall be satisfied.

Blessed are the merciful, for they shall receive mercy.

Blessed are the pure in heart, for they shall see God.

Blessed are the peacemakers, for they shall be called sons of God.

Blessed are those who are persecuted for righteousness' sake, for theirs is the kingdom of heaven.

Blessed are you when others revile you and persecute you and utter all kinds of evil against you falsely on my account. Rejoice and be glad, for your reward is great in heaven, for so they persecuted the prophets who were before you.

# ABOUT THE AUTHOR

Alan Bixler is a native of Missouri and spent most of his formative years in Springfield. He graduated from Central Bible College with Youth Ministry and Bible Degrees, and later from Evangel University with a Master's Degree in Organizational Leadership. In 2019, Alan earned a Doctorate Degree in Strategic Leadership through Regent University.

Alan and his wife, Heather, have been married twenty-seven years and moved from Florida to Sioux Falls, South Dakota in November of 2013 to serve as lead pastors for Crosswalk Community Church.

With a love for people and a passion for helping others find life-direction in Jesus Christ, Alan uses the Bible to challenge and inspire those who desire to develop a deeper understanding of Jesus' available leadership and influence in their everyday lives.

Alan and Heather have two married children. Their daughter Sierra and her husband Cameron Elmore, and their son Hunter and his wife and Kyla Bixler are highly involved in occupational ministry. They serve the Lord in their churches, and through staff leadership roles.

The question Alan and Heather are often asked is, "How long before there are grandkids?" Their response is always, "Hopefully, sooner than later!"

The Bixlers love spending time outdoors with family and friends. Occasionally when they have free time, you may find them biking, kayaking, hunting, fishing, or enjoying time somewhere on a lake, beach, or boat.

You can view Alan's sermons at www.crosswalkcc.com.

# References and Citations

1. Page 5: www.shakespeare-online.com

2. Page 16: https://www.merriam-webster.com/dictionary/beatus

3. Page 18: Jamieson, R., Fausset, A. R., & Brown, D. (1997). Commentary Critical and Explanatory on the Whole Bible. Oak Harbor, WA: Logos Research Systems, Inc.

4. Page 51: Barclay, W. (2001). The Gospel of Matthew (Third Ed., p. 115). Edinburgh: Saint Andrew Press.

5: Page 56: https://www.verywellhealth.com/changing-nutritional-needs-1132088

6. Page 63: Barclay, W. (2001). The Gospel of Matthew (Third Ed., pp. 118–119). Edinburgh: Saint Andrew Press.

7. Page 87: Barclay, W. (2001). The Gospel of Matthew (Third Ed., pp. 126–127). Edinburgh: Saint Andrew Press.

8. Page 102-103: Barclay, W. (2001). The Gospel of Matthew (Third Ed., pp. 128–132). Edinburgh: Saint Andrew Press

9. Page 104-105: Barclay, W. (2001). The Gospel of Matthew (Third Ed., pp. 128–132). Edinburgh: Saint Andrew Press.